C000056113

MATHS FRAMEWORKING

Tiers 6–8

SATs RevisionGuides

Complete Success for Mathematics at KS3

William Collins' dream of knowledge for all began with the publication of his first book in 1819. A self-educated mill worker, he not only enriched millions of lives, but also founded a flourishing publishing house. Today, staying true to this spirit, Collins books are packed with inspiration, innovation and practical expertise. They place you at the centre of a world of possibility and give you exactly what you need to explore it.

Collins. Do more.

Published by Collins
An imprint of HarperCollins*Publishers*
77–85 Fulham Palace Road
Hammersmith
London
W6 8JB

Browse the complete Collins catalogue at
www.collinseducation.com

© HarperCollins*Publishers* Limited 2005

10 9 8 7 6 5 4 3 2 1

ISBN 0 00 721161 9

Kevin Evans, Keith Gordon, Trevor Senior and Brian Speed assert their moral rights to be identified as the authors of this work

British Library Cataloguing in Publication Data.

A Catalogue record for this publication is available from the British Library

Commissioned by Marie Taylor
Project managed by Jenny Wong
Editorial support by Vicky Butt
Edited by Anita Clark
Proofread by Amanda Whyte and Vicky Butt
Design and typesetting by JPD
Covers by Chi Leung
Additional Illustration by Tony Wilkins
Production by Natasha Buckland

Printed and bound by Martins the Printers, Berwick-upon-Tweed

The publishers would like to thank the many teachers and advisers whose feedback helped to shape *Maths Frameworking*.

Every effort has been made to contact the holders of copyright material. But if any have been inadvertently overlooked, the Publishers will be pleased to make the necessary arrangements at the first opportunity.

Contents

How to use this book   **4**

NUMBER   **Level**

1	Significant figures, approximation	**6**	7
2	Negative numbers	**8**	6
3	Fractions	**10**	6, 7
4	Percentages	**12**	6
5	Percentage and proportional change	**14**	6, 7
6	Harder percentages	**16**	8
7	Ratio	**18**	6
8	Powers and roots	**20**	6, 7, 8
9	Standard form	**22**	8

ALGEBRA

10	Number patterns and generalisation	**24**	6
11	Formulae and equations with powers	**26**	7, 8
12	Solving linear equations	**28**	6
13	Linear and simultaneous equations	**30**	8
14	Combining and rearranging alegbraic expressions	**32**	6, 7, 8
15	Expansion of brackets	**34**	7, 8
16	Factorising	**36**	7
17	Substitution	**38**	6, 7
18	Proof and explanation	**40**	7
19	Graphs of linear equations	**42**	6
20	Graphs from real-life	**44**	8
21	Solving inequalities	**46**	7

SHAPE, SPACE AND MEASURES

22	Compound measures	**48**	7
23	Angles in a polygon	**50**	7
24	Pythagoras' theorem	**52**	7
25	Trigonometry	**54**	8
26	Circumference and area of a circle	**56**	6
27	Circles, sectors and cylinders	**58**	8
28	Area of plane shapes	**60**	6
29	Volume of 3-D shapes	**62**	6, 7
30	Congruent and similar shapes	**64**	8
31	Transformations	**66**	6, 7, 8
32	Parallel lines	**68**	6
33	Constructions and loci	**70**	7

HANDLING DATA

34	Probability	**72**	6
35	Relative frequency	**74**	7
36	Probability of combined events	**76**	8
37	Surveys and questionnaires	**78**	6
38	Discrete and grouped data	**80**	6, 7
39	Pie charts	**82**	6
40	Scatter diagrams and lines of best fit	**84**	6, 7
41	Median and mean	**86**	6, 7
42	Stem-and-leaf diagrams and box plots	**88**	6, 7, 8
43	Cumulative frequency	**90**	8
	Answers	**92**	

How to use this book

Each double page covers one topic from the National Curriculum.
You will find the following features on each section.

Section title

This is the particular topic covered in the section.

Exercise number

This will help you find the answers at the back of the book.

Topic area

This is one of the four topic areas of the National Curriculum.

Level

This shows you the assessment level for the topic.

Marks per question

This will show you how to gain marks for your method.

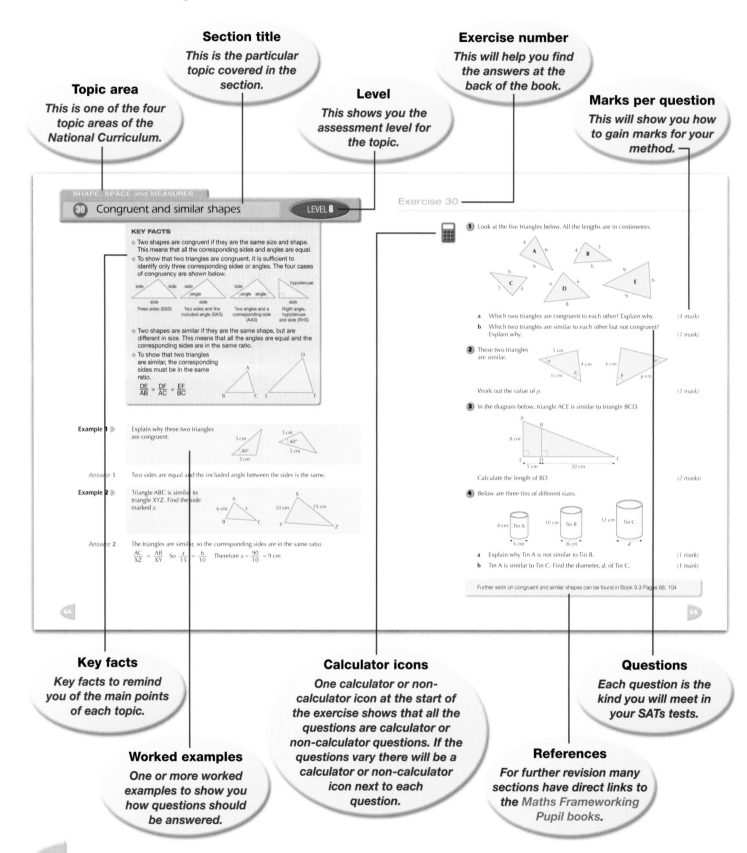

Key facts

Key facts to remind you of the main points of each topic.

Worked examples

One or more worked examples to show you how questions should be answered.

Calculator icons

One calculator or non-calculator icon at the start of the exercise shows that all the questions are calculator or non-calculator questions. If the questions vary there will be a calculator or non-calculator icon next to each question.

References

For further revision many sections have direct links to the *Maths Frameworking Pupil books*.

Questions

Each question is the kind you will meet in your SATs tests.

The National Curriculum tests or SATs

There are four tiers at which you can sit the tests:

- Tier 3–5
- Tier 4–6
- Tier 5–7
- Tier 6–8

Your teachers usually decide which tier you will be entered at. Make sure you know which one is your tier!

In each tier you take two written papers and a mental test.

- Paper 1 is a non-calculator paper.
- Paper 2 is a calculator paper.
- Mental test

Look for this icon.

All three papers have a total mark of 150. Usually you need about 90 marks in total to get the middle grade of each tier.

This book covers the written papers for tiers 6–8.

SATs topics

There are four Attainment Targets (ATs) in the National Curriculum:

- Number
- Algebra
- Shape, Space and Measures
- Handling Data

Each AT is divided into many different topics. These topics are covered in this book.

If there is a particular AT you have difficulty with, look it up in the contents page. You should work through all of the topics in that AT. If there are just a few topics you want extra help with, again use the contents page to find them.

On each section you will find a list of key facts and some worked examples. These may be enough to remind you of the main points of the topic. If you need more help, most sections have a reference to where you can find the topic in the *Maths Frameworking Pupil Books*.

SATs questions

In this book, all of the exercise questions will prepare you for your exams as they are in the style of the National Tests. The worked examples also show you typical questions and how they should be answered.

The number of marks for each question is shown. When you check your answers, you can see if you gained any part marks for showing correct methods. Always remember to show your working – you can still gain marks even if you do not get the correct answer.

Each topic shows the level at which it is assessed. If the topic covers more than one level, then the questions in the exercise will start with the lowest level and finish at the highest level.

Revision

Be sensible with revision.

Focus on what you are not sure about.

Don't leave it until the last minute.

If you don't understand something, ask your teacher.

If you use this book properly then you should gain the highest grade possible.

Best of luck with your tests!

KEY FACTS

- A number to one significant figure will have only one non-zero digit. Zeros in the number are used to show the correct place value: 70, 500, 0.008.
- A number to two significant figures will have two non-zero digits together: 17, 460, 12 000, 1.9.
- Round up or down depending upon the next number after the final significant digit: 5 or more round up; under 5 round down.

Example 1 ▷ The width of a tile is 400 mm, correct to the nearest millimetre.

   a **i**   What is the least possible width of one tile?

      ii   What is the greatest possible width of one tile?

   b Five tiles are fixed to a wall to make a border. What is the least possible width of this border?

←———— width ————→

Answer 1   **a** **i**   The smallest measure that could be rounded up to 400 mm is 399.5 mm.

      ii   The largest measure that could be rounded down to 400 mm is 400.4999 recurring mm. (The 'recurring' is important.)

   b The smallest possible width of one tile is 399.5 mm. The minimum width of the border is therefore $5 \times 399.5 = 1997.5$ mm.

Example 2 ▷ A steam train used to run from Edinburgh to Kings Cross.

The train would travel at a steady 55 miles per hour and use 1 gallon of water for every 350 yards travelled.

Calculate how many gallons of water the train would have used in one hour of travelling. (There are 1760 yards in a mile.)

   a Write down the full calculator display.

   b Now write down your answer correct to two significant figures.

Answer 2   **a** In 1 hour the train would have travelled 55 miles. Find how many yards this is by multiplying 55 by 1760. Then divide this figure by the total number of yards travelled per gallon of water: $55 \times 1760 \div 350 = 276.57143$ gallons.

   b 280 gallons

Exercise 1

 1 The weight, to one significant figure, of one chocolate egg is 50 grams.

    a **i** What is the least possible weight of one chocolate egg? *(1 mark)*

        ii What is the greatest possible weight of one chocolate egg? *(1 mark)*

    b Billie buys eight chocolate eggs.

        What is the least possible total weight of Billie's eggs? *(1 mark)*

 2 The pie chart shows how people spend their earnings each month.

The sum of the percentages is not 100%.

Explain how this can happen if there is no mistake in the pie chart.

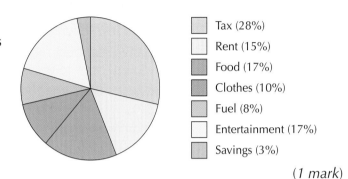

- Tax (28%)
- Rent (15%)
- Food (17%)
- Clothes (10%)
- Fuel (8%)
- Entertainment (17%)
- Savings (3%)

(1 mark)

 3 Write down the approximate answers to one significant figure for the following problems.

Show your working.

    a $\dfrac{205 \times 487}{19}$ *(1 mark)*

    b $798 \times 107 \times 0.487$ *(1 mark)*

 4 **a** Circle the best estimate of the answer to $83.7 \div 7.11$.

        8   9   10   11   12   13 *(1 mark)*

    b Circle the best estimate of the answer to 45.6×0.32.

        0   4.5   9   15   45   90 *(1 mark)*

    c Estimate the answer to $\dfrac{32.16 - 7.72}{2.93}$ giving your answer to 1 significant figure. *(1 mark)*

    d Estimate the answer to $\dfrac{31.7 \times 18.9}{8.68 \times 5.83}$. *(1 mark)*

5 **a** Use your calculator to work out

$$\frac{6.7 + \sqrt{6.7^2 - 4 \times 1.2 \times 5.6}}{2 \times 1.2}$$

        Show all the digits in your calculator display. *(1 mark)*

    b Write your answer to 2 significant figures. *(1 mark)*

Further work on rounding and significant figures can be found in Book 9.1 Page 104
Book 9.2 Pages 32, 105
Book 9.3 Pages 37, 126

2 Negative numbers

KEY FACTS

- Negative numbers are also called directed numbers.
- When answering questions involving negative numbers, it is useful to draw a number line if there isn't one in the question.

$$-9 \ -8 \ -7 \ -6 \ -5 \ -4 \ -3 \ -2 \ -1 \ \ 0 \ \ 1 \ \ 2 \ \ 3 \ \ 4 \ \ 5 \ \ 6 \ \ 7 \ \ 8 \ \ 9$$

- Always start counting at zero on a number line.
- Negative numbers move to the left or down and positive numbers move to the right or up.
- Two signs the same together (+ + or – –) are equivalent to a single plus: $+4 - -5 = +9$, $-3 + +6 = +3$
- Two different signs together (+ – or – +) are equivalent to a single minus: $-3 - +6 = -9$, $+5 + -6 = -1$
- Multiplying or dividing two positive numbers or two negative numbers gives a positive answer: $-2 \times -3 = +6$, $-3 \div -2 = +1.5$
- Multiplying or dividing two numbers with different signs gives a negative answer: $-4 \times +3 = -12$, $+6 \div -2 = -3$

Example 1 Look at the following list of numbers: –8, –6, –3, –1, 3, 6, 8, 9

a What is the total of all eight numbers in the list?

b Choose the three numbers from the list which have the lowest possible total. Do not use the same number more than once.

c Choose three numbers from the list to make the following calculation true:
$$... + ... + ... = 0$$

Answer 1 **a** The total is 8 (or +8).
The calculation can be made easier by grouping numbers together so they cancel each other out: $(-8 + 8) + (-6 + -3 + 9) + -1 + 3 + 6 = 8$

b The smallest total is given by adding the three smallest numbers which are the three negative numbers –8, –6 and –3. Therefore: $-8 + -6 + -3 = -17$

c There are two possible answers: $-6 + -3 + 9 = 0$ or $-8 + -1 + 9 = 0$

Exercise 2

1 a A number machine maps the number n to the number $n - 5$.
Fill in the missing values.

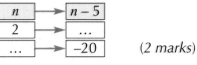

(2 marks)

b A number machine maps the number n to the number $-5n$.
Fill in the missing values.

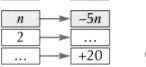

(2 marks)

2 Fill in the blank boxes using only negative numbers to give the value 20.

a ☐ × ☐ = 20   **b** ☐ − ☐ = 20   (2 marks)

3 a Two numbers **multiply** together to make –12 and they **add** together to make 1. What are the two numbers?   (2 marks)

b Two numbers **multiply** together to make +12 and **add** together to make –8. What are the two numbers?   (2 marks)

c 6 squared is 36. The square of another number is also 36.
What is the other number?   (1 mark)

4 Work out the following.

a +7 – +9 = ……   **b** –8 – +7 = ……   **c** –5 + –3 = …….

d +2 × –8 = ……   **e** –24 ÷ –3 = ……   **f** +8 + –6 × +3 = ……   (6 marks)

5 Look at these number cards.

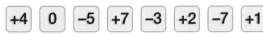

a Choose a card to give the answer 6. +2 + –3 + ☐ = 6   (1 mark)

b Choose a card that gives the **lowest** possible answer. Fill in the card and the answer. –5 + ☐ =   (1 mark)

c Choose a card that gives the **lowest** possible answer. Fill in the card and the answer. –5 – ☐ =   (1 mark)

d Choose two cards that give the answer 0. ☐ + ☐ = 0   (1 mark)

Further work on negative numbers can be found in Book 8.1 Page 2
Book 8.2 Page 2
Book 8.3 Page 2

(3) Fractions

KEY FACTS

- Fractions can only be added or subtracted if they have the same denominator. If you are asked to add or subtract fractions with different denominators, you must find the lowest common denominator:

$$\frac{2}{3} + \frac{1}{5} = \frac{10}{15} + \frac{3}{15} = \frac{13}{15}, \quad \frac{3}{4} - \frac{2}{5} = \frac{15}{20} - \frac{8}{20} = \frac{7}{20}$$

- When multiplying fractions, cancel by any common factors top and bottom before multiplying the numerators and denominators.

$$\frac{3}{4} \times \frac{2}{9} = \frac{\cancel{3}^{1}}{\cancel{4}_{2}} \times \frac{\cancel{2}^{1}}{\cancel{9}_{3}} = \frac{1}{6}$$

- When dividing by a fraction, turn it upside down and multiply by it.

$$\frac{2}{9} \div \frac{1}{3} = \frac{2}{\cancel{9}_{3}} \times \frac{\cancel{3}^{1}}{1} = \frac{2}{3}$$

- When adding and subtracting mixed numbers, separate the whole numbers and the fractions and deal with them separately.

- When multiplying and dividing mixed numbers make them into top heavy fractions first.

Example 1

a A farmer is selling a field for building.

Company A buys $\frac{1}{10}$ of the field.
Company B buys $\frac{1}{4}$ of the field.
Company C buys $\frac{2}{5}$ of the field.
Company D buys the rest of the field.
What fraction of the field does company D buy?

b Another farmer is selling a field for building divided into 20 equal plots.
One plot costs £20 000.
A company buys $\frac{3}{5}$ of the plots.
How much do they pay?

Answer 1

a Between them companies A, B and C buy $\frac{1}{10} + \frac{1}{4} + \frac{2}{5}$ of the field.

You need to add these fractions together, so first find the lowest common denominator of 10, 4 and 5: 20.

Next, change all the fractions into twentieths: $\frac{1}{10} + \frac{1}{4} + \frac{2}{5} = \frac{2}{20} + \frac{5}{20} + \frac{8}{20}$

And then add the numerators: $= \frac{15}{20}$

The whole field is equal to 1, so subtract the total from 1: $1 - \frac{15}{20} = \frac{5}{20}$

Finally, answer the question, simplifying your answer:
Company D buys $\frac{5}{20} = \frac{1}{4}$ of the field.

b $\frac{3}{5}$ of 20 plots $= \frac{3}{5} \times 20 = \frac{3}{5} \times \frac{20}{1} = 12$

12 plots cost $12 \times £20\,000 = £240\,000$

Exercise 3

1 **a** Work out the area of this triangle. *(3 marks)*

b How many of these triangles will fit into a rectangle that is 4 cm by 10 cm? *(2 marks)*

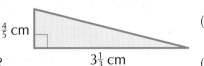

$\frac{4}{5}$ cm

$3\frac{1}{3}$ cm

2 Work out the following.

a $\frac{4}{5} - \frac{1}{4}$ **b** $2\frac{3}{8} + 1\frac{2}{3}$ **c** $1\frac{3}{5} \times \frac{15}{16}$ **d** $2\frac{2}{9} \div 1\frac{2}{3}$ *(4 marks)*

3 The fraction $\frac{3}{8}$ is halfway between $\frac{1}{4}$ and $\frac{1}{2}$.

What fraction is halfway between the following?

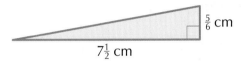

$\frac{1}{4}$ $\frac{3}{8}$ $\frac{1}{2}$

a $\frac{1}{8}$ and $\frac{1}{4}$ **b** $\frac{1}{3}$ and $\frac{5}{6}$ *(2 marks)*

4 A square has an area that is eight times the area of the triangle below.

$\frac{5}{6}$ cm

$7\frac{1}{2}$ cm

What is the side of the square? *(2 marks)*

5 Work out the following.

a $2\frac{2}{3} + 1\frac{1}{4}$ **b** $2\frac{1}{5} - 1\frac{1}{3}$ **c** $1\frac{3}{4} \times 1\frac{3}{5}$ **d** $2\frac{3}{5} \div 1\frac{1}{5}$ *(4 marks)*

6 Work out the following.

a $\left(\frac{2}{3}\right)^2$ **b** $\sqrt{\frac{9}{25}}$ **c** $\sqrt{\frac{4}{9}} \times \left(\frac{3}{5}\right)^2$ *(3 marks)*

7 The rule for continuing a sequence is:

     Multiply by 2 and add $\frac{1}{5}$

The first three terms of a sequence starting with 2 are as follows:

     $2, 4\frac{1}{5}, 8\frac{3}{5}, \ldots$

Work out the next two terms of the sequence. *(2 marks)*

8 Work out the following.

a $\left(2\frac{1}{4} + 1\frac{1}{5}\right) \times 1\frac{2}{3}$ **b** $\left(3\frac{1}{2} \div 2\frac{5}{8}\right) + 1\frac{2}{3}$ *(4 marks)*

Further work on fractions can be found in Book 9.2 Pages 16, 18, 169
Book 9.3 Pages 18, 197

4 Percentages

KEY FACTS

o Change a fraction to a percentage by multiplying it by 100.

For example: $\frac{4}{5} = \frac{4}{5} \times 100$ (cancel down the 5 and the 100)

which gives $\frac{4}{\not{5}_1} \times \not{100}^{20} = 4 \times 20 = 80\%$

o To find A as a percentage of B, calculate the fraction then multiply by 100.

For example, to calculate £6 as a percentage of £20, express as a fraction:

$\frac{6}{20}$, then multiply by 100. $\frac{6}{20} \times 100 = 30\%$

o Change a decimal to a percentage by multiplying by 100.

For example, 0.6 as a percentage = 0.6 × 100 = 60%.

Example 1 ▷ Joy asked 60 children which colour they liked best.

a   Which colour did 50% of the boys like best?

b   Which colour did 15% of the girls like best?

c   Joy said: "In my survey, green was just as popular with boys as with girls." Explain why Joy was wrong.

d   Which colour was equally popular with boys and girls?

Colour	Number of boys	Number of girls
Blue	10	13
Red	3	9
Yellow	5	10
Pink	0	6
Green	2	2
	20	**40**

Answer 1

a   Blue. 50% is a half. 10 is half of 20.

b   Pink. There are 40 girls in total. 15% of 40 = (10% + 5%) of 40 = 4 + 2 = 6.

c   The number of boys who like green is 2 out of 20 which is 10%. The number of girls who like green is 2 out of 40 which is 5%.

d   Yellow. 5 out of 20 boys liked yellow which is 25%. 10 out of 40 girls liked yellow which is 25%.

Example 2 ▷ Calculate the missing numbers.

a   15%   of   £60   =   £ [   ]

b   15%   of   [£   ]   =   £6

c   [%]   of   £80   =   £16

Answer 2

a   15% of £60 = 15 × 60 ÷ 100 = £9.

b   If 15% represents £6, then 5% (15% ÷ 3) represents £2 (£6 ÷ 3).
So 10% (5% × 2) represents £4 (£2 × 2).
So 100% (10% × 10) represents £40 (£4 × 10).
Hence 15% of **£40** = £6.

c The question is really asking: "What percentage of £80 is £16?"
In other words, what percentage is the fraction $\frac{16}{80}$.
This is found by multiplying the fraction by 100.
So, $16 \div 80 \times 100 = 20\%$.

Exercise 4

1 The table shows some percentages of amounts of money.

	£10	£70	£105
5%	50p	£3.50	£5.25
10%	£1	£7	£10.50

Use the table to work out the missing numbers.

a £10.50 = 15% of £ _____   *(1 mark)*

b £7.50 = _____ % of £10   *(1 mark)*

c £1.75 = 5% of £ _____   *(1 mark)*

2 The table shows the 2004 population of each of the world's continents.

a Which continent had approximately 8% of the world's population in 2004? *(1 mark)*

b In 2004, what percentage of the world's population was living in Asia? *(2 marks)*

Continent	Population (in millions)
Australia	31
Africa	823
Antarctica	0
Asia	3737
Europe	729
North America	486
South America	351
World total	**6157**

3 A report on the number of MPs in the UK in 2004 found: "There are 659 MPs. About 18% of them are women."

a The percentage was rounded to the nearest whole number, 18.
Which of the numbers below is the smallest value the percentage could have been, to one decimal place?

17.1%	17.2%	17.3%	17.4%	17.5%
17.6%	17.7%	17.8%	17.9%	18.0%

(1 mark)

b What is the smallest number of women MPs that there might have been in 2004? (Use your answer to part **a** to help you calculate this answer.) *(2 marks)*

Further work on percentages can be found in Book 8.1 Page 45
Book 8.2 Page 47
Book 8.3 Page 54

5 Percentage and proportional change LEVEL 6, 7

KEY FACTS

○ When a value, V, is increased or decreased by a percentage, P, the formula is:

$$\text{New value} = V(1 \pm \frac{P}{100})$$

○ The quantity $1 \pm \frac{P}{100}$ is called a multiplier and is useful when calculating with percentages.

○ To work out a proportional change, calculate the value of one item. For example, if seven books cost £41.79, what is the cost of 12 books?

Calculate the cost of one book: £41.79 ÷ 7 = £5.97.

Now calculate the cost of 12 books: 12 × £5.97 = £71.64.

This is called the Unitary Method.

Example 1 ▷ 1 kilogram (1 kg) ≈ 2.2 pound weight (2.2 lb). 1 pound weight (1 lb) = 16 ounces (16 oz).

    a How many ounces is 5 kg?   **b** How many grams is 1 lb?

Answer 1   **a** 5 kg = 5 × 2.2 lb = 11 lb
          11 lb = 11 × 16 oz = 176 oz

     b 1 lb = 1 kg ÷ 2.2
          1 kg = 1000 g
          1000 g ÷ 2.2 ≈ 455 g

Example 2 ▷ In 1996, 81 755 400 passengers travelled by air in and out of the UK.

In 2002, 105 677 600 passengers travelled by air in and out of the UK.

Calculate the percentage increase in air passengers in the UK between 1996 and 2002.

Answer 2 The actual increase is 105677600 − 81755400 = 23922200.

The percentage increase is $\frac{23922200}{81755400} \times 100 = 29.26\%$.

Exercise 5

1 **a** A standard pack of dishwasher powder contains 1 kg of powder.
      The recommended amount for one wash is 40 g of powder.
      How many washes can you get from one packet of powder?   *(1 mark)*

    b A special offer pack contains 20% more powder than a standard pack.
      How many washes can you get from a special offer pack?   *(1 mark)*

2 Winston's journey to work is normally 18 miles.

   a A road diversion increases the distance by 35%. How far is this journey? *(2 marks)*

   b On the way home Winston takes another route which is 4 miles longer than his normal route. What percentage of 18 miles is 4 miles? *(2 marks)*

3 £1 = $1.80 (US dollars). £1 = €1.40 (Euros).

   a How much is £2.55 in US dollars? *(1 mark)*

   b How much is €4.50 in pounds? *(1 mark)*

   c How many Euros will you get for $558 (US dollars)? *(2 marks)*

4 The cost of a Breezyjet Airlines flight depends on how soon before you intend to fly you book a ticket.

Time of booking	Percentage of full fare
Within 1 week	100%
1–2 weeks	85%
2 weeks–1 month	65%
1–2 months	50%
2–3 months	40%
Over 3 months	30%

   a A Breezyjet flight from Luton to Nice has a full fare of £160. How much will the fare be if you book 2 months 2 weeks before the flight time? *(2 marks)*

   b A Breezyjet flight from Liverpool to Dublin has a full fare of £68. John pays £44.20. When did he book the flight? *(2 marks)*

5 **a** In 1975 the price of a VW beetle car was £1440 and sales tax was charged at 15%. How much tax would a customer have paid? *(2 marks)*

   b In 2005 the price of a VW beetle is £10 682 including sales tax of £1282. What percentage of the price is tax? *(2 marks)*

6 **a** Which of these calculations gives the answer to the question: What is 14% of £56?

     14×56 0.14×56 1.14×56 1.4×56 *(1 mark)*

   b Which of these gives the answer to the question: What is 14 increased by 56%?

     56×14 0.56×14 1.56×14 5.6×14 *(1 mark)*

   c Fill in the missing value.

     To increase a quantity by 15% multiply by … *(1 mark)*

7 In 1901 the population of Leeds was 552 479. In 2001 it was 715 404. What is the percentage increase in the population of Leeds between 1901 and 2001? *(2 marks)*

Further work on proportional change can be found in Book 9.1 Page 29

Book 9.2 Page 21

Book 9.3 Page 21

6 Harder percentages

KEY FACTS

- To calculate a percentage increase, the multiplier is found by adding the percentage increase expressed as a decimal to 1.

  For example, to increase £200 by 3%, the multiplier is given by $1 + 0.03 = 1.03$. So the new total = £200 × 1.03 = £206.

- To calculate a percentage decrease, the multiplier is found by subtracting the percentage decrease expressed as a decimal from 1.

  For example, to decrease 500 grams by 16%, the multiplier is given by $1 - 0.16 = 0.84$. So the new total = £500 × 0.84 = £420.

- Repeated percentage changes, for example compound interest, can be calculated using multipliers.

  For example, a coat costs £120. The price is increased by 15%. In a sale the new price is then reduced by 8%. What is the price in the sale?

  The multiplier for a 15% increase = 1 + 0.15 = 1.15.
  The multiplier for an 8% decrease = 1 − 0.08 = 0.92.
  The new price = £120 × 1.15 × 0.92 = £126.96.

- To calculate a percentage increase or decrease use the formula:

  $$\text{Percentage change} = \frac{\text{change}}{\text{original}} \times 100\%$$

  For example, the price of a DVD player is reduced from £95 to £76.
  What is the percentage decrease?

  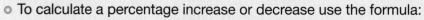

  Decrease = £95 − £76 = £19.
  Percentage decrease = $\frac{19}{95} \times 100\% = 20\%$

- To calculate a reverse percentage is to work out an original quantity.

  For example, a shirt is reduced by 10% in a sale. The sale price is £15.30.

  What was the price before the sale?
  The sale price = 100% − 10% = 90% of the original price.

  So 0.90 × original price = sale price.

  0.90 × original price = £15.30

  Original price = £15.30 ÷ 0.90 = £17.00

Example 1 Which of the following is the multiplier used to calculate a 3% decrease?

0.7   1.03   0.97   1.3

Answer 1 3% = 0.03
1 − 0.03 = 0.97

Exercise 6

1 **a** Which one of the calculations below gives the correct answer to the question: 'What is 60 decreased by 4%?'

60×0.4 60×1.4 60×0.04 60×0.96 60×0.6 *(1 mark)*

b Fill in the missing decimal number:
To increase by 13%, multiply by ......   *(1 mark)*

2 An antique increases in value by 25% in one year. It is now worth £20 000. How much was it worth one year ago?   *(2 marks)*

3 **a** A car was priced at £6000 in 2004.
In 2005 the price was increased by 8%.
In 2006 the price was increased by 8%

Which of these expressions show the cost of the car in 2006?

6000×0.08^2 $6000 \times 1.08 \times 2$ $(6000 \times 0.08)^2$

$6000 \times 1.0 \times 2$ 6000×1.08^2 $(6000 \times 1.08)^2$ *(1 mark)*

b In 2004 car insurance was £p.
In 2005 the cost of the insurance was increased by 10%.
In 2006 the cost of the insurance was decreased by 12%.
Write down an expression that shows the cost of the insurance in 2006.   *(1 mark)*

4 A 10% increase followed by a 20% increase is not the same as a total increase of 30%. What is the total percentage increase?
Show your working.   *(1 mark)*

5 The price of a litre of petrol is 87p.

a Copy and complete the following table to show the percentage of the price that goes to retailers, taxes and others. Show your working.

5p retailers

61p taxes

21p other

Retailers	%
Taxes	%
Others	%

(2 marks)

b The percentages for diesel are as follows.

Retailers	7%
Taxes	74%
Others	21%

If the retailer receives 6p, what is the cost of one litre of diesel?   *(2 marks)*

Further work on percentages can be found in Book 9.2 Pages 21, 23
Book 9.3 Pages 21, 24

7 Ratio

KEY FACTS

○ Ratios are simplified by cancelling by the highest common factor in the same way as cancelling fractions.
For example, £10 : £15 = 2 : 3 (divide both numbers by 5).
Note that there are no units in the answer.

○ Ratios are often written in the form 1 : n.
For example, 4 : 9 = 1 : 2.25 (divide both numbers by 4).

○ When dividing a quantity in a given ratio, first add up the total number of parts, then work out what one part is worth and finally multiply this amount by each of the ratios.

Example 1 ▷ A drink is made from orange juice and lemonade in the ratio 2 : 5.
How much lemonade is needed if 100 ml of orange juice is used?

Answer 1 The ratio of orange juice to lemonade must cancel down to 2 : 5.
100 : x = 2 : 5, so each number needs to be multiplied by 50 to give x = 5 × 50 = 250.
250 ml of lemonade is needed.

Example 2 ▷ Anne and Dave divide £40 between them in the ratio 3 : 5.
How much does each person receive?

Answer 2 The ratio 3 : 5 means that there are 3 + 5 = 8 equal parts.
So 1 part = £40 ÷ 8 = £5.
Anne receives £5 × 3 = £15 and Dave receives £5 × 5 = £25.

Exercise 7

1 Write each of the following ratios in its simplest form.

    a   4 : 12   **b**   9 : 15   **c**   14 : 49   **d**   36 : 48   *(4 marks)*

2 Write each of the following ratios in the form 1: n.

    a   2 : 7   **b**   4 : 10   **c**   5 : 8   **d**   10 : 27   *(4 marks)*

3 The ratio of the weights of the two cereal packets is 2 : 3.
Find the weight in the larger packet.   *(2 marks)*

4   **a**   In Andy's class, there are 14 boys and 16 girls.
         Write down the ratio of boys to girls in its simplest form.   *(1 mark)*

    b   In Joan's class the ratio of boys to girls is 4 : 5.
        How many boys are in the class, if there are 15 girls?   *(1 mark)*

5 **a** Divide £80 in the ratio 1 : 4. *(2 marks)*

b Divide 120 kg in the ratio 3 : 7. *(2 marks)*

6 Copy and shade the diagram so that the ratio of shaded squares to unshaded squares is 3 : 5.

(2 marks)

7 In a wood there are oak trees, beech trees and sycamore trees in the ratio 1 : 2 : 3.

Find the number of each type of tree if there are 600 trees in the wood. *(2 marks)*

8 As a Christmas present, Grandma Wilson decides to share out £60 between her two grandchildren in the ratio of their ages.

a How much does each child receive, if Hannah is 4 years old and Jack is 6 years old? *(2 marks)*

b The following Christmas she shares out £60 again in the ratio of their ages.

How much does each child receive on the following Christmas? *(2 marks)*

9 The design below is made from two grey squares and one black square.

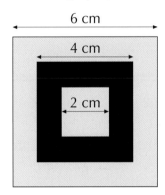

Find the ratio of the black area to the grey area, giving your answer in its simplest form. *(3 marks)*

10 A supermarket sells tins of baked beans in two sizes.

The small tin costs 25p and the large tin costs 40p.

a Write down the ratio of the weights of the two tins in its simplest form. *(1 mark)*

b Write down the ratio of the cost of the two tins in its simplest form. *(1 mark)*

c Which tin gives the better value for money? *(2 marks)*

Further work on ratio can be found in Book 8.3 Page 189
Book 9.1 Page 27
Book 9.2 Page 26

Powers and roots

LEVEL **6, 7, 8**

KEY FACTS

○ $3^4 = 3 \times 3 \times 3 \times 3 = 81$. (3 is the base number and 4 is the power or index.)

On a calculator use the $\boxed{y^x}$ key.

○ Laws of indices: $x^a \times x^b = x^{a+b}$ (add the indices)

$x^a \div x^b = x^{a-b}$ (subtract the indices)

$(x^a)^b = x^{ab}$ (multiply the indices)

$x^0 = 1$

$x^{-1} = \frac{1}{x}$ (the reciprocal of x)

$x^{-a} = \frac{1}{x^a}$

○ $\sqrt{25} = 5$ or -5, because $5 \times 5 = 25$ or $-5 \times -5 = 25$. This is written as ± 5.

On a calculator use the $\boxed{\sqrt{x}}$ key.

○ $\sqrt[3]{27} = 3$, because $3 \times 3 \times 3 = 27$.

On a calculator use the $\boxed{\sqrt[3]{x}}$ key.

Example 1 ▷ Which is the bigger number, 4^5 or 5^4?

Answer 1 $4^5 = 1024$ and $5^4 = 625$, so 4^5 is the bigger number.

Example 2 ▷ Write the following as decimals.

a 1.2^3 b $\sqrt{0.49}$ c $\sqrt[3]{0.008}$ d 10^{-1} e 2^{-3}

Answer 2 a 1.728 b ± 0.7 c 0.2 d $\frac{1}{10} = 0.1$ e $\frac{1}{2^3} = \frac{1}{8} = 0.125$

Exercise 8

1 Work out the following.

a 2^7 b 3^6 c 10^8 (*3 marks*)

2 Work out the following, leaving your answer in index form.

a $4^3 \times 4^5$ b $5^8 \div 5^2$ c $(7^3)^4$ (*3 marks*)

3 Put these numbers in order of size:

$\sqrt[3]{27}$ 2^4 $\sqrt[3]{125}$ 3^{-2} 3^0 (*5 marks*)

4 Solve the following equations.

    a $x^2 = 16$ **b** $x^2 - 7 = 93$ **c** $2x^2 + 8 = 26$ *(6 marks)*

5 Solve the following equations.

    a $x^3 = 64$ **b** $x^3 - 1 = 26$ **c** $4x^3 - 10 = 22$ *(3 marks)*

6 Here are some number cards.

    a Which number is the largest?   *(2 marks)*

    b Which number is equal to 8^2?   *(1 mark)*

7 **a** Find the values of a and b.

        $625 = 25^a = 5^b$ *(2 marks)*

    b Find the values of m and n.

        $2^m \times 3^n = 72$ *(2 marks)*

8 For each of these cards n can be any number.

    a If $n > 1$, which card will always give an answer greater than n?   *(1 mark)*

    b If $n < 0$, which card has no answer?   *(1 mark)*

    c What value of n gives the same answer for all of the cards?   *(1 mark)*

9 Some numbers are greater than their squares.

For example: $0.5 > 0.5^2$

Which numbers are equal to their squares?   *(2 marks)*

10 $\sqrt{12}$ lies between 3 and 4, since $3^2 = 9$ and $4^2 = 16$.

Find two consecutive whole numbers that each of the following lies between:

    a $\sqrt{40}$ **b** $\sqrt{90}$ **c** $\sqrt{200}$ *(3 marks)*

11 This cube has a volume of $100\ m^3$.
Find the length of each side, s, giving
your answer to one decimal place.   *(1 mark)*

12 **a** Substitute different values for x and y to show that

        $\sqrt{x} \times \sqrt{y} = \sqrt{xy}$ *(2 marks)*

    b Substitute different values for x and y to show that

        $\sqrt{x} + \sqrt{y} \neq \sqrt{x + y}$ *(2 marks)*

Further work on powers and roots can be found in Book 9.1 Pages 102, 118
                                              Book 9.2 Pages 121, 123
                                              Book 9.3 Page 140

9 Standard form

KEY FACTS

○ Standard form is used to write very large or very small numbers in a format that can easily be typed into a calculator. Numbers expressed in standard form are always written as: $a \times 10^n$, where $1 \leq a < 10$ and n is an integer.
For example: $12\,000\,000\,000$ is written as 1.2×10^{10} and $0.000\,074$ is written as 7.4×10^{-5}

○ On most calculators, you use the EXP button to key in a number in standard form.

For example: the number 7×10^8 is keyed in as 7 EXP 8

and the number 5×10^{-7} is keyed in as 5 EXP 7 ±

Example 1 ▷ The Earth, on average, is 9.3×10^7 miles from the Sun.

Light travels at a speed of 1.86×10^5 miles per second.

How long does it take a ray of light to travel from the Sun to the Earth? Give your answer to the nearest minute.

Answer 1 Time $= \dfrac{\text{Distance}}{\text{Speed}} = \dfrac{9.3 \times 10^7}{1.86 \times 10^5} = 500$ seconds $= 8$ minutes 20 seconds
$= 8$ minutes to the nearest minute.

Example 2 ▷ The mass of an electron is 9.11×10^{-31} kg and the mass of a proton is 1.67×10^{-27} kg.

How many times heavier is the proton? Give your answer to 2 significant figures.

Answer 2 $\dfrac{1.67 \times 10^{-27}}{9.11 \times 10^{-31}} = 1800$ (2 significant figures).

Exercise 9

1 The planet Mars has two Moons, Phobos and Deimos.

Deimos is 2.35×10^6 km from the centre of Mars.

Phobos is 9.38×10^5 km from the centre of Mars.

a What is the minimum distance between the two Moons?

Give your answer in standard form.

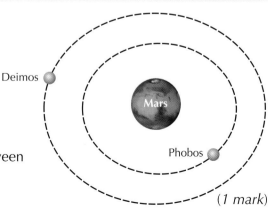

(1 mark)

b What is the maximum distance between the two Moons?
Give your answer in standard form. *(1 mark)*

2 $\frac{1}{4000}$ is equal to 0.00025

    a Write 0.00025 in standard form. *(1 mark)*

    b Write $\frac{1}{40\,000}$ in standard form. *(1 mark)*

    c Work out $\frac{1}{4000} + \frac{1}{40\,000}$, giving your answer in standard form. *(1 mark)*

3 The table shows information about five continents.

Continent	Population	Area (km²)
Africa	8.07×10^8	3.01×10^7
Asia	3.70×10^9	4.46×10^7
Europe	7.31×10^8	9.94×10^6
North America	4.81×10^8	2.43×10^7
South America	3.50×10^8	1.78×10^7

    a Which continent has the largest population? *(1 mark)*

    b Which continent has the smallest area? *(1 mark)*

    c Which of Africa or North America has the greater number of people per km²? *(3 marks)*

4 Below is some information about the Earth and the Moon.

Mass of the Earth $= 5.98 \times 10^{24}$ kg
Mass of the Moon $= 7.35 \times 10^{22}$ kg
Distance between the Earth and the Moon $= 3.89 \times 10^5$ km

The gravitational force, F, between the Earth and the Moon can be calculated by using the formula:

$$F = \frac{Gm_1m_2}{R^2}$$

where $m_1 =$ the mass of the Earth,
$m_2 =$ the mass of the Moon,
$R =$ the distance between them
and $G =$ the gravitational constant $= 6.67 \times 10^{-20}$

Use the formula to calculate the gravitational force between the Earth and the Moon.
Give your answer in standard form to 3 significant figures. *(2 marks)*

5 The Earth's orbit is roughly circular and the distance from the Earth to the Sun on average is 9.3×10^7 miles.

    a Write down what the following calculations represent.

        i $2\pi \times 9.3 \times 10^7$ *(1 mark)*

        ii $\dfrac{2\pi \times 9.3 \times 10^7}{365 \times 24}$ *(1 mark)*

    b Work out $\dfrac{2\pi \times 9.3 \times 10^7}{365 \times 24}$, giving your answer to the nearest hundred. *(1 mark)*

Further work on standard form can be found in Book 9.3 Pages 120, 123, 125

KEY FACTS

- Each number in a sequence is called a term.
- Each term has a position in the sequence. For example, 1st, 2nd, 3rd, 4th.
- The value of a term can be found by using its position in the sequence. For example, the nth term in the sequence 1, 2, 3, 4, … is n; the nth term in 3, 6, 9, 12, … is $3n$; the nth term in 1, 4, 9, 16, … is n^2.
- Sequences can be described by a 'term-to-term' rule or by an algebraic rule (nth term).
- If a sequence increases by the same value each time, the nth term will be of the form $an + b$, where a is the constant incremental value. For example, the sequence 3, 7, 11, 15, … increases by 4 each time. The nth term is $4n + b$, to find b add or subtract to get the first term, so $4 - 1 = 3$, giving $b = -1$.
- Two special sequences are the square numbers (1, 4, 9, 16, 25, 36, …) and the triangle numbers (1, 3, 6, 10, 15, 21, …).

Example 1 ▷ Trevor is making rectangular patterns with black, grey and white square tiles. He uses black tiles for the corners, grey tiles for the edges and white tiles for the middle.

a Complete the table to show how many tiles of each colour are used in a 4 by 6 rectangle.

b Trevor makes a rectangle using five white tiles for the middle. How many grey tiles will the rectangle have?

c Trevor now makes a rectangle using 24 white tiles for the middle. Explain why you cannot say how many grey tiles the rectangle will have.

Colour	Number
Black	
Grey	
White	
Total	24

d Trevor has four black tiles, 14 grey tiles and 12 white tiles. If he uses **all** of the tiles there is only one rectangle that he can make. Draw the rectangle.

Answer 1

a There are four black tiles, 12 grey tiles and eight white tiles.
Check that these total 24: $4 + 12 + 8 = 24$.

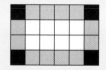

b As 5 is a prime number it can only be arranged in a 1 by 5 rectangle.

There will be 12 grey tiles.

c As 24 can be arranged in a 1 by 24, a 2 by 12, a 3 by 8 and a 4 by 6 rectangle you do not know which size has been chosen.

d Although the 12 white tiles could be formed into three different middles (1 by 12, 2 by 6 or 3 by 4) there is only one middle (3 by 4) that uses 14 grey tiles.

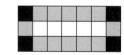

Exercise 10

1 The table shows the counting numbers arranged in a five-column grid.

a Which column will the number 78 be in? *(1 mark)*

b Column 1 forms the sequence 1, 6, 11, 16, 21, ...
What number in this sequence will be in the tenth row? *(1 mark)*

	Col 1	Col 2	Col 3	Col 4	Col 5
Row 1	1	2	3	4	5
Row 2	⑥	7	8	9	10
Row 3	11	⑫	13	14	15
Row 4	16	17	⑱	19	20
Row 5	21	22	23	㉔	25
Row 6					

c The nth term of the numbers in the fourth column is $5n - 1$.
What is the nth term of the numbers in column 3? *(1 mark)*

d The numbers in the 6 times table are shown circled.
Row 1 does not contain any numbers in the 6 times table.
Which is the next row that does not contain any numbers in the 6 times table? *(1 mark)*

2 The nth term of a sequence is given by the rule: 'Square the number n and add 1'.
For $n = 1, 2, 3, 4, ...$ this generates the sequence: 2, 5, 10, 17, ...

a Work out the value of the 100th term of the sequence. *(1 mark)*

b Write down an expression for the nth term of the sequence. *(1 mark)*

c Use this expression to help you find how many numbers in the sequence are less than 900. *(1 mark)*

3 Hexagons can be made from matches.

 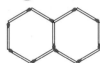  

1 hexagon	2 hexagon	3 hexagon	4 hexagon
6 matches	11 matches	16 matches	21 matches

Which of the following expressions shows the number of matches, M, needed for H hexagons?

$H = 6M$ $\qquad$ $H = 6M + 5$ $\qquad$ $H = 5M + 1$ $\qquad$ $H = 5M - 1$ *(1 mark)*

4 The pyramid of numbers below is built up row by row.

```
                1                    Row 1
             2  3  4                 Row 2
          5  6  7  8  9              Row 3
      10 11 12 13 14 15 16           Row 4
```

a An expression for the middle number in row n is $n^2 - n + 1$.
Write an expression for each of the following:
  i the number on the right side of the middle number *(1 mark)*
  ii the number on the left side of the middle number. *(1 mark)*

b Calculate the middle number in row 12. *(1 mark)*

c Write an expression for the last number in row n. *(1 mark)*

Further work on number patterns and generalisation can be found in Book 9.1 Pages 2–10
Book 9.2 Pages 2, 5, 13
Book 9.3 Pages 2, 5, 46

11 **Formulae and equations with powers** **LEVEL 7, 8**

KEY FACTS

○ Powers occur in many equations and formulae in mathematics.
For example:

Volume of cone = $\frac{1}{3}\pi r^2 h$;

Surface area of a sphere = $4\pi r^2$

○ Powers must always be evaluated first, according to the rules of BODMAS.

Example 1 ▷ For each card n can be any positive number. $\sqrt[3]{n}$ $\boxed{3n}$ $\boxed{\dfrac{n}{3}}$ $\boxed{n^3}$ $\boxed{\dfrac{3}{n}}$

   a Which expression gives the greatest value when n is between 0.5 and 1?

   b Which expression gives the greatest value when n is between 3 and 4?

   c Which expression gives the greatest value when n is between –1 and –2?

Answer 1   **a** Try 0.5 and 1 in each expression. $\frac{3}{n}$ gives answers between 6 and 3.
6 is the greatest possible answer when $n = 0.5$.

   b Try 3 and 4 in each expression. n^3 gives 64 when $n = 4$, which is the greatest possible answer.

   c Try –1 and –2 in each expression. $\frac{n}{3}$ gives $-\frac{1}{3}$ when $n = -1$ which is the greatest possible answer.

Example 2 ▷ **a** Find the values of a and b when $p = 20$.

   i $a = \dfrac{2p^3}{5}$ **ii** $b = \dfrac{3p^2(p-5)}{25}$

   b Simplify these expressions.

   i $\dfrac{6a^2 b^3}{9ab^2}$ **ii** $\dfrac{9x^3 y^2}{15x^2 y^5}$

Answer 2   **a** **i** $a = \dfrac{2 \times 20^3}{5} = \dfrac{2 \times 8000}{5} = \dfrac{16\,000}{5} = 3200$

    ii $b = \dfrac{3 \times 20^2 \times (20-5)}{25} = \dfrac{3 \times \overset{16}{\cancel{400}} \times 15}{\underset{1}{\cancel{25}}} = 3 \times 16 \times 15 = 720$

   b **i** $\dfrac{\overset{2}{\cancel{6}} \times \cancel{a} \times a \times \cancel{b} \times \cancel{b} \times b}{\underset{3}{\cancel{9}} \times \cancel{a} \times \cancel{b} \times \cancel{b}} = \dfrac{2ab}{3}$

    ii $\dfrac{\overset{3}{\cancel{9}} \times \cancel{x} \times \cancel{x} \times x \times \cancel{y} \times \cancel{y}}{\underset{5}{\cancel{15}} \times \cancel{x} \times \cancel{x} \times \cancel{y} \times \cancel{y} \times y \times y \times y} = \dfrac{3x}{5y^3}$

Exercise 11

1 A formula connecting three variables a, b and c is $a = 12 + b(10 - c)^2$.

    a Work out the value of b when $a = 2$ and $c = 5$.   *(1 mark)*

    b Work out the **values** of c when $a = 36$ and $b = 6$.   *(2 marks)*

2 The SUVAT equations are used to calculate variables when a body moves with constant acceleration. They connect:

    s the distance travelled in m u the initial speed in m/s
    v the final speed in m/s a the acceleration in m/s^2
    t the time taken in seconds

The equations are: $v = u + at$ $v^2 = u^2 + 2as$ $s = ut + \frac{1}{2}at^2$

    a For a particular journey, $u = 2$ m/s, $t = 5.5$ s and $a = 2$ m/s^2.
        Use the appropriate equations to find:
        i   the distance travelled   **ii**   the final velocity.   *(2 marks)*

    b For another journey, $u = 10$ m/s, $v = 4$ m/s and $s = 6$ metres.
        i   Use the appropriate equation to calculate the acceleration.   *(1 mark)*
        ii   Explain what this answer tells you about the acceleration.   *(1 mark)*

3 Formulae for working out the perimeter (P) and area (A) of a shape like this are:

$$P = x + y + \frac{5}{3}\sqrt{(x^2 - y^2)}$$
$$A = \left(\tfrac{1}{2}y - \tfrac{1}{9}\right)\sqrt{(x^2 - y^2)}$$

    a Work out P and A when $x = 13$ and $y = 12$.   *(2 marks)*

    b Work out P and A when $x = 8.5$ and $y = 8.4$.   *(2 marks)*

    c Substitute $x = 5t$ and $y = 3t$ into the formulae to work out the perimeter and area of this shape.   *(2 marks)*

4 An annulus has a volume (V) and a surface area (S) given by the following formulae: $V = \pi h(b^2 - a^2)$
                                   $S = \pi(b + a)(2h + b - a)$

    i   Work out the volume and surface area of an annulus with
           $h = 3.2$, $b = 4.5$, $a = 3.6$.   *(2 marks)*

    ii   Substitute $h = 3a$ and $b = 3a$ to work out the volume and
           surface area of an annulus in terms of a and π.   *(2 marks)*

5 For each card n can be any positive number.

    a Which two cards will always give a number bigger than n?   *(2 marks)*

    b When $n = 1$, which two cards will give the answer of 1?   *(2 marks)*

    c When n is less than 1, which card will give an answer less than n?   *(1 mark)*

Further work on formulae and equations with powers can be found in Book 9.2 Page 121
Book 9.3 Page 138

12 Solving linear equations

KEY FACTS

- An equation always contains an equals sign.
- Equations work like a balancing scale. The amount on one side equals the amount on the other side.
- Whatever operation (+, −, × or ÷) is carried out on one side of the equation must also be carried out on the other side of the equation.
- Solving an equation involves finding the value of the unknown letter.

Example 1 ▷ Solve the equation $3m - 5 = 7$.

Answer 1 Add 5 to both sides to give: $3m - 5 + 5 = 7 + 5$

Since $-5 + 5 = 0$ and $7 + 5 = 12$, this simplifies to $3m = 12$

Divide both sides by 3 to find the answer: $m = 4$

Example 2 ▷ Jack is x years old. He says that if he multiplies his age by 3 and subtracts 2, he gets the same answer as when he adds 6 and then doubles his answer.

This equation shows the information: $3x - 2 = 2(x + 6)$

Solve the equation to work out Jack's age.

Answer 2 First, multiply out the bracket: $3x - 2 = 2x + 12$

Next, subtract $2x$ from both sides to give: $3x - 2 - 2x = 2x + 12 - 2x$

Simplify $3x - 2x = x$ and $2x - 2x = 0$, to give: $x - 2 = 12$

Now add 2 from both sides to give: $x - 2 + 2 = 12 + 2$

Therefore, $x = 14$

Exercise 12

1 Look at the following table.

Write in words the meaning of each equation below.

The first one has been done for you.

		Number of pencils
Red		r
Green		g
Blue		b

$r = 7$	The number of red pencils is 7.
$r + g = 11$	
$b = 3r$	
$b - g = 17$	

(3 marks)

2 Solve the following equations. Show your working.

    a $2p + 5 = 9$ *(1 mark)*

    b $6m - 7 = 11$ *(1 mark)*

    c $3y + 5 = y + 17$ *(2 marks)*

    d $10x + 14 = 8x + 13$ *(2 marks)*

3 The following diagram shows a rectangle. The area of the rectangle is 41 cm².

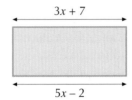

    Calculate the value of x and use it to find the length and width of the rectangle.   *(2 marks)*

4 The diagram below shows some bricks. The bricks on the bottom row add up to the same value as the brick on the top row.

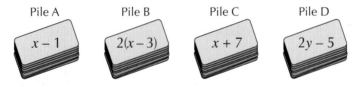

    By writing down an equation, calculate the value of x.   *(2 marks)*

5 Billy has four piles of cards containing $x - 1$, $2(x + 3)$, $x + 7$, $2y - 5$ cards.

    Pile A   Pile B   Pile C   Pile D

    $x - 1$ $2(x - 3)$ $x + 7$ $2y - 5$

    a   The total number of cards in Pile A and B is 23.
          Use this information to set up an equation.
          Then work out the value of x.   *(2 marks)*

    b   The number of cards in Piles C and D are equal.
          Use this information to work out the value of y.   *(1 mark)*

Further work on solving equations can be found in Book 9.1 Pages 43–48, 166
                                               Book 9.2 Pages 37–42, 173
                                                Book 9.3 Page 202

13 Linear and simultaneous equations

KEY FACTS

○ Linear equations at Level 8 will have the variable occurring twice.

○ To solve these equations collect all the letter terms on one side of the equals sign and the number terms on the other side.

○ When terms change sides, they also change signs.

○ Simultaneous equations have two variables which have values that solve both equations at the same time (simultaneously).

○ To solve simultaneous equations either substitute one variable into the other equation or eliminate one variable.

○ Once the value of one variable has been calculated, substitute this value back into one of the original equations to get the value of the other variable.

Example 1 ▷

Three families have a snack in a café.

The Ahmeds have three teas and five sticky buns. It costs them £5.80.

The Browns have four teas and three sticky buns. It costs them £5.35.

The Carrs order five teas and two sticky buns.

Use simultaneous equations to work out the bill for the Carrs.

Let x be the cost of a tea. Let y be the cost of a sticky bun.

Answer 1

Set up the equations.	$3x + 5y = 580$	(1)
	$4x + 3y = 535$	(2)
Multiply (1) by 4	$12x + 20y = 2320$	(3)
Multiply (2) by 3	$12x + 9y = 1605$	(4)
Subtract (3) – (4)	$11y = 715$	
Solve the equation	$y = 65$	
Substitute into (1)	$3x + 325 = 580$	
Solve the equation	$x = 85$	
The Carrs pay	$5 \times 85 + 2 \times 65 = £5.55$	

Example 2 ▷

Look at the following expressions.   **A** $2(x - 3)$ **B** $4(x + 3)$ **C** $3(4 - x)$

a What value of x makes expression A equal to expression B?

b What value of x makes expression A equal to expression C?

c What value of x makes expression B equal to expression C?

Answer 2

a $2(x - 3) = 4(x + 3) \Rightarrow 2x - 6 = 4x + 12 \Rightarrow -18 = 2x \Rightarrow x = -9$

b $2(x - 3) = 3(4 - x) \Rightarrow 2x - 6 = 12 - 3x \Rightarrow 5x = 18 \Rightarrow x = 3.6$

c $4(x + 3) = 3(4 - x) \Rightarrow 4x + 12 = 12 - 3x \Rightarrow 7x = 0 \Rightarrow x = 0$

Exercise 13

1 Both of these rectangles have a perimeter of 20 cm.

 $y + 3$ $x + 2$

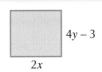 $4y - 3$ $2x$

    a Show that $x + y = 5$ and that $2x + 4y = 13$.   *(2 marks)*

    b Solve the simultaneous equations to find the values of x and y.   *(2 marks)*

2 Solve the following simultaneous equations.

    $y = 2x + 3$ $3y = 8x + 4$ *(3 marks)*

3 Two simultaneous equations are: $y = 2x + 5$ and $3y = x + 5$.

    a Explain why $6x + 15 = x + 5$ *(1 mark)*

    b Solve $6x + 15 = x + 5$ *(1 mark)*

    c Find the value of y.   *(1 mark)*

4 Look at the following two expressions. $4z - 3$ $3z + 4$

    a What value of z makes the two expressions equal?   *(1 mark)*

    b What value of z makes the second expression three times as great as the first?   *(2 marks)*

5 Solve this equation: $\dfrac{4(3y - 1)}{2y} = 3$ *(2 marks)*

6 The diagram shows an equilateral triangle. Use algebra to find the values of a and b.   *(3 marks)*

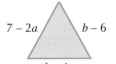

$7 - 2a$ $b - 6$ $b - 4a$

7 Solve the following equations.

    a $4(2x - 1) = 3(x + 2)$ *(2 marks)*

    b $\dfrac{3y - 2}{4} = 2y + 3$ *(2 marks)*

    c $\dfrac{3z + 2}{z} = 7$ *(2 marks)*

8 Three watsits and five spandoliks cost £13.80.

One watsit and three spandolicks cost £6.20.

What is the cost of two watsits and one spandolick?   *(3 marks)*

9 Two families visit the zoo.

The Wilkinsons buy three adult tickets and four child tickets for £44.50.

The Youngs buy two adult tickets and three child tickets for £32.50.

Use simultaneous equations to work out the cost of an adult and a child ticket.   *(3 marks)*

Further work on linear and simultaneous equations can be found in
Book 8.1 Page 119
Book 8.2 Page 121, Book 9.2 Page 37
Book 8.3 Page 134, Book 9.3 Page 42

14 Combining and rearranging algebraic expressions   LEVEL **6, 7, 8**

KEY FACTS

- Numbers in front of letters are called coefficients.
- A single letter has a coefficient (which does not need to be written) of 1, e.g. $a = 1a$.
- $3ab$ and $3ba$ are like terms as $ab = ba$.
- To rearrange a formula use inverse operations.
- When rearranging an expression to make a letter the subject, solve the expression as you would an equation. Unlike an equation, each step gives an algebraic expression rather than a numerical answer.

Example 1 ▷

Here are six cards with algebraic expressions on them.

$2x - 2$	$3x + 4$	$5x + 1$	$2x + 3x$	$2(x - 1)$	$3(x + 2)$
Card **A**	Card **B**	Card **C**	Card **D**	Card **E**	Card **F**

a Which two cards have **equivalent** expressions?

b What algebraic expression do you get from Card **C** – Card **A**?

c The sum of which two cards gives the expression $6x + 10$?

d Explain why there is no value of x so that Card **C** = Card **D**.

Answer 1

a $2(x - 1) = 2x - 2$ when it is expanded, so Card **A** and Card **E** are equivalent.

b $5x + 1 - (2x - 2) = 5x + 1 - 2x + 2 = 3x + 3$

c $3(x + 2) + 3x + 4 = 3x + 6 + 3x + 4 = 6x + 10$, so Cards **B** and **F**.

d If Card **C** = Card **D** then $5x + 1 = 5x$ which is impossible.

Example 2 ▷

Rearrange the formula $A = \pi r^2$, to make r the subject.

Answer 2

Divide both sides by π. $\dfrac{A}{\pi} = r^2$

Square root both sides and reverse the formula. $r = \sqrt{\dfrac{A}{\pi}}$

Exercise 14

1 In these walls each brick is made by adding together the two bricks below it. For example:

11	
5	6

Write the missing expressions in the walls below as simply as possible.

a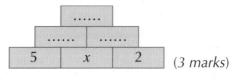

b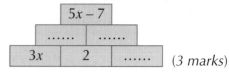

5x − 7

5 | x | 2   *(3 marks)*

3x | 2 | ......   *(3 marks)*

2 Write an expression for the missing lengths in this rectangle.

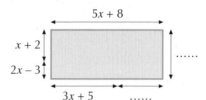

5x + 8

x + 2

2x − 3

......   *(2 marks)*

3x + 5   ......

3 Find the missing expressions to make these equations true.

a 2x + 1 + 4x − 3 = ...   **b** 2x + 1 + (......) = 5x + 4

c 2x + 1 − (......) = x + 4   *(3 marks)*

4 **a** The subject of the following equation is x: x = 3(a + b).
Rearrange the equation to make *a* the subject.   *(2 marks)*

b Rearrange the equation $x = \frac{1}{3}(a − b)$ to make *b* the subject.   *(2 marks)*

5 The perimeter, P, of a semicircle with radius r is given by: P = πr + 2r.

a Factorise πr + 2r.   *(1 mark)*

b Rearrange the formula for the perimeter to make *r* the subject.   *(1 mark)*

r

6 The formula for the volume, V, of a cone of radius r and height h is $V = \frac{1}{3}\pi r^2 h$.
Rearrange the formula to make *r* the subject.   *(2 marks)*

7 This solid is a prism with depth 2x. The volume is $6x^3$.

a Rearrange the formula to make *x* the subject.   *(2 marks)*

b What volume of x will give a volume of 500 cm³?
Give your answer to one decimal place.   *(1 mark)*

8 Make *y* the subject of each of these formulae. Simplify your answer as much as possible.

a 6x − 2 = 10 − 2y   *(2 marks)*   **b** 6x + 15 = 3(y − 4)   *(2 marks)*

9 Make *u* the subject of each of these formulae.

a v = u + at   *(1 mark)*   **b** $v^2 = u^2 + 2as$ *(2 marks)*

10 The volume, V, of a sphere of radius r, is $V = \frac{4}{3}\pi r^3$.

a Rearrange the formula to make *r* the subject.   *(2 marks)*

b What is the radius of a sphere with a volume of 100 cm³?
Give your answer to one decimal place.   *(1 mark)*

Further work on combining and rearranging algebraic expressions can be found in
Book 9.2 Page 162
Book 9.3 Page 192

15 Expansion of brackets

KEY FACTS

○ When two brackets are expanded or multiplied together, each term in the first bracket is multiplied with each term in the second bracket.

For example:

$$(x + 2)(x + 3) = x(x + 3) + 2(x + 3)$$
$$= x^2 + 3x + 2x + 6$$
$$= x^2 + 5x + 6$$

○ One way to remember how to expand two brackets is to use the acronym FOIL:
- multiply together the **F**irst terms in each bracket
- multiply together the **O**uter terms in the brackets
- multiply together the **I**nner terms in the brackets
- multiply together the **L**ast terms in each bracket.

Example 1 ▷ Expand the brackets for the following.

a $(x + 6)(x - 4)$ **b** $(3x - 5)(x + 2)$ **c** $(2x - 3)^2$

Answer 1

a $(x + 6)(x - 4) = x^2 - 4x + 6x - 24 = x^2 + 2x - 24$

b $(3x - 5)(x + 2) = 3x^2 + 6x - 5x - 10 = 3x^2 + x - 10$

c $(2x - 3)^2 = (2x - 3)(2x - 3) = 4x^2 - 6x - 6x + 9 = 4x^2 - 12x + 9$

Example 2 ▷ Show that the area of the rectangle on the right is $x^2 + 9x + 20$ by splitting it into four smaller rectangles.

$x + 5$

$x + 4$

Answer 2

The rectangle can be split as follows:

The area of the rectangle is $(x + 5)(x + 4)$.

This is the same as the area of the four rectangles:

$x^2 + 5x + 4x + 20 = x^2 + 9x + 20$

	x	5
x	x^2	$5x$
4	$4x$	20

Exercise 15

1 Expand the brackets for the following.

a $(a + 6)(a + 3)$ **b** $(b + 1)(b - 4)$ **c** $(c - 6)(c + 7)$

d $(4d - 5)(d - 4)$ **e** $(3e - 2)^2$ **f** $(3 - 2f)(5 + 3f)$ (*12 marks*)

2 a Which expression below is the same as $x^2 + 10x + 24$? *(1 mark)*

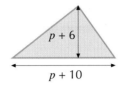

$(x + 2)(x + 3)$ $(x + 3)(x + 8)$ $(x + 2)(x + 12)$

$(x + 4)(x + 6)$ $(x + 2)(x + 8)$

b Multiply out the expression $(2y - 1)(y + 9)$. *(2 marks)*

3 Show that the area of the triangle below is $\frac{1}{2}p^2 + 8p + 30$.

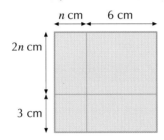

$p + 6$

$p + 10$

(2 marks)

4 The rectangle below is $(n + 6)$ cm long and $(2n + 3)$ cm wide.
It has been split into four smaller rectangles.

n cm   6 cm

$2n$ cm

3 cm

a Find the area of each small rectangle. *(2 marks)*

b Write down the expansion of $(n + 6)(2n + 3)$. *(1 mark)*

5 Liam says:

Show that Liam is wrong.

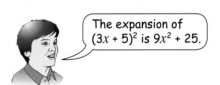

The expansion of $(3x + 5)^2$ is $9x^2 + 25$.

(2 marks)

6 a Show that $(x + y)(x - y) = x^2 - y^2$. *(2 marks)*

b Use this expansion to find each of the following without squaring any numbers.

  i $18^2 - 17^2$ **ii** $45^2 - 35^2$ **iii** $56^2 - 44^2$ *(3 marks)*

Further work on expansion of brackets can be found in Book 9.3 Page 183

16 **Factorising**

LEVEL **7**

KEY FACTS

- ◉ Factors of a number divide exactly into the original number.
  For example, factors of the number 12 are 1, 2, 3, 4, 6 and 12.
- ◉ Factorising is the reverse of multiplying out brackets.
  For example, multiplying out $3(4x + 2) = 12x + 6$;
  factorising $12x + 6 = 3(4x + 2)$.
- ◉ To factorise is to take out common factors from each term.
  For example, the common factors of $3y^2 - 6y$ are 3 and y.
  Factorising $3y^2 - 6y = 3y(y - 2)$.

Example 1 ▷ The box contains six expressions.
Write down the equivalent pairs.

| $2x + 6$ | $x^2 + 6x$ | $x(x + 6)$ |
| $x^2 + 3x$ | $2(x + 3)$ | $x(x + 3)$ |

Answer 1 $2x + 6 = 2(x + 3)$ $x^2 + 6x = x(x + 6)$ $x^2 + 3x = x(x + 3)$

Example 2 ▷ Prove that the sum of two different even numbers is always even.

Answer 2 Let the even numbers be $2n$ and $2m$.
  Sum $= 2n + 2m = 2(n + m)$

This is a multiple of 2, so it must be even.

Exercise 16

1 Which of the following are **not** factors of both $18a^2b$ and $12ab^2$?

$3ab$ $6a$ $2a^2b^2$ $18ab$ $3b$ (*1 mark*)

2 a Which two of the expressions below are equivalent?

$4(3a + 5)$ $3(4a + 20)$ $3(4a + 9)$

$7(a + 9)$ $2(6a + 30)$ (*1 mark*)

b Which one of the expressions below is a correct factorisation
of $20b - 5$?

$4(5b - 1)$ $2(10b - 3)$ $5(15b - 1)$

$5(4b - 1)$ $5(4b - 4)$ (*1 mark*)

3 Which one of the expressions below is the odd one out? Explain your answer.

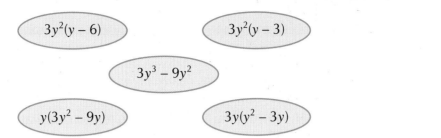

$3y^2(y-6)$

$3y^2(y-3)$

$3y^3 - 9y^2$

$y(3y^2 - 9y)$

$3y(y^2 - 3y)$

(1 mark)

4 **a** Factorise the following expression.

$4x + 12 = $ ....

(1 mark)

b Factorise the following expression as fully as possible.

$10x^3 - 5x^2 = $ ....

(1 mark)

5 The diagram below shows a parallelogram.

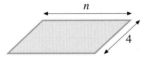

Alan says the perimeter is $2n + 8$. Beth says the perimeter is $2(n + 4)$.
Which of the following statements is correct?

Both Alan and Beth are right.   Both Alan and Beth are wrong.
Alan is right and Beth is wrong.   Alan is wrong and Beth is right.   *(1 mark)*

6 Shaun thinks that the sum of three consecutive integers is always
a multiple of 3.

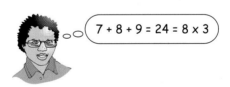

7 + 8 + 9 = 24 = 8 × 3

Use algebra to show that he is right.   *(2 marks)*

7 **a** Simplify $n + n + 1 + n + 2 + n + 3$.   *(1 mark)*

b Factorise $4n + 6$.   *(1 mark)*

c Prove that the sum of four consecutive numbers is even.   *(1 mark)*

Further work on factorising can be found in Book 9.2 Page 119
Book 9.3 Page 186

17 Substitution

LEVEL **6, 7**

KEY FACTS

○ Substitution involves replacing variables with values in an algebraic formula.

○ When substituting into a formula, remember that the rules of BODMAS still apply.

○ Rules of algebra need careful attention. For example,
$3a = 3 \times a$, $a^2 = a \times a$, $\frac{a}{2} = a \div 2$, $3a^2 = 3 \times a^2$

Example 1 ▷ The formula for the approximate temperature conversion from degrees Fahrenheit (F) into degrees Celsius (C) is: $C = \frac{1}{2}(F - 32)$.

a Find C when F = 68°.

b Find C when F = 20°.

Answer 1 **a** $C = \frac{1}{2} \times (68 - 32) = \frac{1}{2} \times 36 = 18°C$

b $C = \frac{1}{2} \times (20 - 32) = \frac{1}{2} \times (-12) = -6°C$

Example 2 ▷ The formula for finding the longest side (or hypotenuse), h, of a right-angled triangle, given the two shorter sides a and b is
$$h = \sqrt{a^2 + b^2}$$

a Find h when $a = 8$ cm and $b = 6$ cm.

b Find h when $a = 3.5$ m and $b = 2.8$ m.

Answer 2 **a** $h = \sqrt{8^2 + 6^2} = \sqrt{64 + 36} = \sqrt{100} = 10$ cm

b $h = \sqrt{3.5^2 + 2.8^2} = \sqrt{12.25 + 7.84} = \sqrt{20.09} = 4.5$ m (1 dp)

Exercise 17

1 Use the formula $y = x^2 + 5$ to find y when:

a $x = 6$ **b** $x = -3$ **c** $x = 2.5$ (*3 marks*)

2 Use the formula $a = \dfrac{2b^2 - 4}{2}$ to find a when:

a $b = 4$ **b** $b = -2$ **c** $b = 1.6$ (*3 marks*)

3 The formula $F = \dfrac{9C + 32}{5}$ is the exact conversion to convert temperatures from degrees Celsius, C, into degrees Fahrenheit, F.

Use the formula to find the Fahrenheit temperature for each of the following.

    a   The freezing point of water: 0°C.

    b   The boiling point of water: 100°C.

    c   The normal body temperature: 37.1°C.

    d   The temperature of a freezer: –8°C.   *(4 marks)*

4 The cost of a phone call is calculated by using the formula:

$$P = \dfrac{t + 30}{20}$$

where P is the cost in pence and t is the length of the call in seconds.

    a   Jane is on the phone for 5 minutes. Calculate the cost of her call.   *(2 marks)*

    b   John makes a phone call which costs 9p. How long was he on the phone?   *(2 marks)*

5 The cost to enter a theme park is given by the formula: $E = 8.5a + 4.5c$, where E is the entry cost, a is the number of adults and c is the number of children.

    a   Calculate the cost for six children and three adults to enter the park.   *(2 marks)*

    b   Mr and Mrs Hardy and their children go to the park and the cost is £35. How many children do Mr and Mrs Hardy have?   *(2 marks)*

6 The formula for finding the sum, S, of the first n positive numbers, $1 + 2 + 3 + 4 + \ldots\ldots + n$, is given by:

$$S = \dfrac{n(n + 1)}{2}$$

Use the formula to find the sum of:

    a   the first 10 positive numbers   **b**   the first 50 positive numbers

    c   the first 1000 positive numbers.   *(3 marks)*

7 The formula for finding the velocity, v, in metres per second, of an object is given by:

$v = \sqrt{u^2 + 2as}$ where u is the initial velocity, a is the acceleration and s is the distance travelled.

Calculate v for the following, giving your answer to one decimal place.

    a $u = 10$, $a = 3$ and $s = 40$ *(2 marks)*

    b $u = 40$, $a = -4$ and $s = 20$ *(2 marks)*

Further work on substitution can be found in Book 9.1 Page 38

Book 9.2 Page 161

(18) Proof and explanation

KEY FACTS

- If you are asked to provide a proof or an explanation for a mathematical statement you need to adopt a logical approach.
- You should always give a reason for anything you write down and should never expect the marker to assume something just because it is 'obvious'.
- Try to use mathematical symbols and notation rather than words. For example, use the symbol ':.' for 'therefore' and '⇒' for 'it follows that'.
- Keep explanations short if you have to use words and use the correct mathematical vocabulary.
- Look for a 'clue' in the number of marks. For example, 1 mark usually means a single statement, 2 marks usually requires two statements and so on.

Example 1 ▷

P is a prime number and Q is an odd number.

For each part of the question, choose the statement that is true.

a   PQ is always odd   **b**   P(Q–1) is always odd

      PQ is always even   P(Q–1) is always even

      PQ could be odd or even   P(Q–1) could be odd or even

Answer 1

a   Although most prime numbers are odd, there is one even prime number, 2.

     ∴   PQ could be odd × odd = odd or even × odd = even,

     ⇒ PQ could be odd or even.

b   If Q is odd, then Q – 1 is even, no matter what value P has.

     ∴   P(Q – 1) is odd × even or even × even,

     ⇒ P(Q – 1) is always even.

Example 2 ▷

Prove that there is only one triangle that:

   Has one right angle

   Has a perimeter of 12 cm

   Has three sides that are all whole numbers in centimetres

Answer 2

As the perimeter of the triangle is 12 cm and the sides have to be whole centimetres, the sides could only be either 2 cm, 5 cm, 5 cm or 3 cm, 4 cm, 5 cm or 4 cm, 4 cm, 4 cm.

If the triangle has a right angle, the sides will obey Pythagoras' theorem.

$$5^2 + 2^2 \neq 5^2, \; 4^2 + 4^2 \neq 4^2, \text{ but } 3^2 + 4^2 = 5^2$$

Hence, the triangle with sides 3 cm, 4 cm and 5 cm obeys all three conditions.

Exercise 18

1 n is an integer.

Say whether each of the following statements is true or false.

Give an example each time to justify your choice.

    a $n(n + 1)$ is always odd   *(1 mark)*

    b $n(n+1)(n + 2)$ is always even   *(1 mark)*

    c $n^2 + 1$ can be odd or even   *(1 mark)*

2 For each part of the question, write down the statement that is true.

    a **i**   When x is odd, x^2 is odd.   **ii**   When x is odd, x^2 is even.

           Show how you know it is true for all odd values of x.   *(1 mark)*

    b **i**   When x is odd, $(x - 1)(x + 1)$ is odd.

       ii   When x is odd, $(x - 1)(x + 1)$ is even.

           Show how you know the statement is true for all odd values of x.   *(1 mark)*

3 This is part of Sandra's homework. $\dfrac{40.7 \times 56.5}{32.7 - 8.3} = 94.2$ (to 1 dp)

By using estimation decide whether or not the answer could be right.
Show your calculations.   *(3 marks)*

4 For each of the following statements, find a value for x that makes that
statement true.

    a $x^2 < x$ **b** $x^2 = x$ **c** $x^2 > x$ *(3 marks)*

5 A quadrilateral can be split into two triangles.
A pentagon can be split into three triangles.

    a   What is the angle sum of an octagon?   *(1 mark)*

    b   Explain why the following rule is true for the angle sum of a
        n-sided polygon.

        Angle sum = $(n - 2) \times 180$ *(2 marks)*

6 **a**   Explain why you cannot make a triangle using the three sticks
        shown below.

        —————————————   —————   ———

                9 cm   5 cm   3 cm   *(1 mark)*

    b   Think about triangles that have:

        A perimeter of 13 cm
        Two equal sides
        Each side a whole number of centimetres

        Prove that there are only three possible triangles that obey all
        three rules.   *(2 marks)*

19 Graphs of linear equations

KEY FACTS

○ An equation is a formula that is true for all points on a graph. For example, on the graph of $y = 2x$, the y coordinate is always double the x coordinate.

○ A linear equation can be written in the form $y = mx + c$: for example, $y = 3x + 5$. It can also be written in the form $ax + by = c$: for example, $x + y = 6$.

○ m is the gradient, which is a measure of how steep the line is and c is the y intercept, i.e. the point where the graph crosses the y-axis.

Example 1 ▷

The graph on the right shows a straight line.

a In the table below, write the coordinates of four points on the line. Then complete the table by calculating $x + y$.

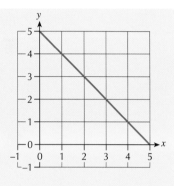

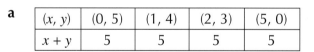

(x, y)	(,)	(,)	(,)	(,)
$x + y$				

b Write down the equation of the straight line.

c On a new grid, draw two straight lines with equations $x = 3$ and $y = 2$.

Write down the coordinates of the point where the two lines cross.

Answer 1

a

(x, y)	(0, 5)	(1, 4)	(2, 3)	(5, 0)
$x + y$	5	5	5	5

b The equation is $x + y = 5$.

c

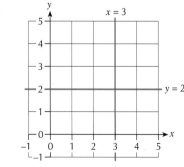

The coordinates of the point where the two lines cross is (3, 2).

Exercise 19

1 This graph shows a straight line.
The equation of the line is $y = 2x + 1$.

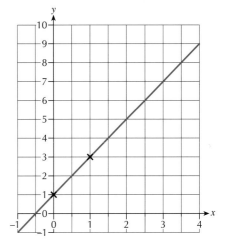

   a Does the point (20, 41) lie on the
straight line?
Explain how you know. *(1 mark)*

   b Write down the coordinates of
the point where the line $y = 6$
meets the line $y = 2x + 1$. *(1 mark)*

   c Write down the equation of a
line that is parallel to the line
$y = 2x + 1$. *(1 mark)*

2 The admission price to a cinema is £5.10 per person.

   a Copy and complete the following table.

Number of people	0	10	20	30
Total cost of admission	0	£51		

(1 mark)

   b Draw a graph to show this information. Join the points with a
straight line. *(2 marks)*

   c Use your graph to work out the total cost of admission for 25 people. *(1 mark)*

3 **a** Copy the graph below and write the equations of each line. *(4 marks)*

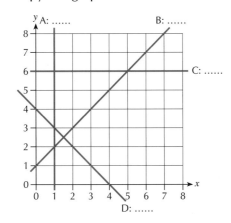

   b Which **two** lines will meet the line $y = 2x$ at the same point?
Explain your answer. *(1 mark)*

Further work on graphs of linear equations can be found in

Book 9.1 Pages 13, 123, 157
Book 8.2 Pages 85, 87, Book 9.2 Page 164
Book 8.3 Page 93

KEY FACTS

- Real-life graphs can be used to show realistic everyday situations in a graphical way.
- Examples include distance–time graphs, velocity–time graphs and graphs that show the heights of objects thrown in the air.
- The graphs model the real-life situation. This means that they give a broad view of what is happening and not an exact representation.
- Always look at the axes to determine exactly what information is being shown.
- Read scales carefully.

Example 1 ▷ Jenny hits a golf shot of 180 metres. Which graph shows the path of the shot?

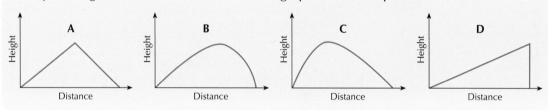

Answer 1 Graph B. The ball is given an initial velocity which is partly overcome by air resistance so it falls to the ground faster.

Graphs A and D are unrealistic as objects do not pass through the air in straight lines. Graph C is unrealistic as it implies the ball was given some forward velocity after it reached the highest point.

Example 2 ▷ Mr Speed does a 10 kilometre run that takes him 50 minutes.

The distance–time graph shows his progress.

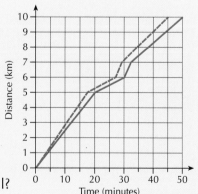

a What is his average speed in kilometres per hour?

b At one point Mr Speed runs up and down a very steep hill of length 1 km.

    i How many kilometres from the start of the run is the hill?

    ii How long does it take him to run **down** the hill?

c The next week Mr Speed does the same run and increases his average speed by 30 seconds a kilometre.

    Draw a possible distance–time graph to show this run.

Answer 2   **a** 12 kilometres per hour. 10 kilometres in 50 minutes is 1 kilometre every 5 minutes.

b i The hill started at 5 km. We can see this on the graph as the line becomes less steep, showing that he slowed down.

ii The line on the graph steepens sharply at 6 km. The next kilometre is covered in $2\frac{1}{2}$ minutes.

c A possible answer is shown dotted on the graph. The key points are that it is above the previous graph and that it ends at 45 minutes.

Exercise 20

1 The graph shows the journeys of two cyclists racing from Ashville to Barton and back.

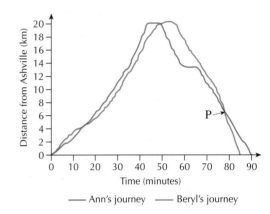

Ann's journey —— Beryl's journey

a Barton is 20 km from Ashville. Who was in the lead when they reached Barton? *(1 mark)*

b Who won the race and by how many minutes? *(1 mark)*

c Ann waited at Barton for Beryl. For approximately how many minutes was she waiting? *(1 mark)*

d Ann had a puncture on the way back. Approximately how long did it take her to mend it? *(1 mark)*

e Describe what happened at point P. *(1 mark)*

2 Frank throws a ball horizontally from the top of a cliff.

Which of the following graphs shows the path of the ball?

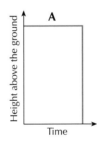 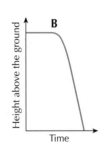 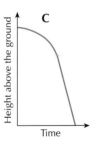 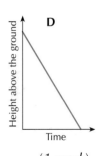

(1 mark)

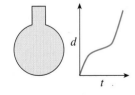

3 The graph shows how the depth, *d*, of the container increases with time, *t*, as a steady flow of water is poured into it. The container is shown in cross section.

Draw graphs to show how the depth of these containers increases as water is poured in steadily.

a 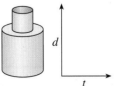 **b** 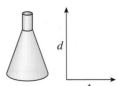 **c**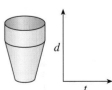

(3 marks)

Further work on real life graphs can be found in Book 8.3 Page 98
Book 9.2 Pages 77, 125
Book 9.3 Page 88

21 Solving inequalities

KEY FACTS

- $<$ (less than) and $>$ (greater than) are strict inequalities because they do not include the boundary. For example, $x < 3$ means x can take any value less than 3 but not 3 itself.

- $\leq$ (less than or equal to) and $\geq$ (greater than or equal to) mean that the boundary point is included. For example, $x \geq 3$ means x can take any value greater than 3 and 3 itself.

- Inequalities can be shown on number lines. A strict inequality would have an open circle as the boundary and an inclusive inequality would have a shaded circle as the boundary.

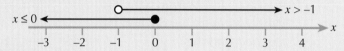

- Graphical inequalities such as $y \leq 2x + 3$ give a region on one side of the boundary line $y = 2x + 3$.

- A strict graphical inequality such as $2x + 3y > 6$ would have a dotted boundary line to show that it is not included.

Example 1

Four points are $A(3, 1)$, $B(4, 1)$, $C(2, 5)$, $D(2, 1)$.

Write down the point or points that obey the inequalities given.

The first line is done for you.

	Inequality	Points
	$x > 2$ is true for points	A, B
a	$y < 3$ is true for points	
b	$x + y \geq 4$ is true for points	
c	$y + 2x > 6$ is true for points	

Answer 1

a   The y coordinate is the second value. It is less than 3 for points A, B and D.

b $x + y$ is the sum of both coordinates. $x + y \geq 4$ for points A, B and C.

c $y + 2x$ is double the first coordinate plus the second.
    $y + 2x > 6$ for points A, B and C.

Example 2

A teacher wants her class to find a point on the grid by asking questions about inequalities.

Use the questions and the answers in the table to identify the point.

Question	Answer
Is $x > 0$?	No
Is $x + y > 1$?	Yes
Is $y < 3$?	Yes

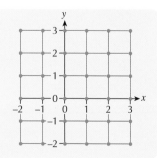

Answer 2

If x is not greater than 0, then all points to the right of the y axis are eliminated.
If $x + y$ is greater than 1 then the only points that are true are $(0, 2)$, $(0, 3)$, $(-1, 3)$.
If $y < 3$ the only point from the three above is $(0, 2)$.
Hence the point is $(0, 2)$.

1 The number line below shows the set of numbers $-2 < x \le 3$.

a Write down the set of numbers shown on this number line.

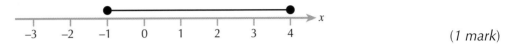

(1 mark)

b Write down the set of numbers shown on this number line.

(1 mark)

c Write down an integer that is in both sets of numbers in parts **a** and **b**.

(1 mark)

2 a Solve the equation $2x + 7 = 13$. *(1 mark)*

b Which of the following is the solution to the inequality $2x + 7 > 13$?

$x \ge 3$ $\qquad$ $x < 3$ $\qquad$ $x > 3$ $\qquad$ $x \le 3$ *(1 mark)*

c Which of the following is the solution to the inequality $7 - 2x > 13$?

$x > -3$ $\qquad$ $x < 3$ $\qquad$ $x > 3$ $\qquad$ $x < -3$ *(1 mark)*

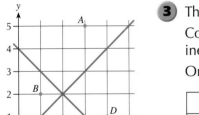

3 The graph shows the lines $y = x$ and $x + y = 4$.

Copy and complete the table below with the points that obey the inequalities at the top of each row and at the side of each column.

One has been done for you.

	$x + y > 4$	$x + y < 4$
$y > x$	A	
$y < x$		

(3 marks)

4 If $n^2 < 25$ then n is between -5 and $+5$. So $-5 < n < 5$.

Write down the solution set to the following inequalities.

a $n^2 \le 36$ $\qquad$ **b** $n^2 < 100$ *(2 marks)*

5 If $n^2 \ge 4$, then n is bigger than or equal to 2 or smaller than or equal to -2.

So $n \ge 2$ or $n \le -2$.

Write down the solution set to the following inequalities.

a $n^2 \ge 9$ $\qquad$ **b** $n^2 > 25$ *(2 marks)*

6 Solve the inequalities **a** $x - 5 > 13$ **b** $5x + 1 \le 11$ **c** $3 - 2x < 5$. *(3 marks)*

Further work on solving inequalities can be found in Book 9.3 Page 50

KEY FACTS

○ Speed is a measure of how fast an object is moving. To calculate speed, two measurements are needed: distance and time. Usually, an 'average speed' is calculated over the total distance travelled.

○ Common units of speed are: metres per second (m/s), kilometres per hour (km/h) and miles per hour (mph).

A formula triangle can be used to show the connection between distance (D), speed (S) and time (T).

Covering up the quantity required leads to the formulae:

$$D = ST \qquad S = \frac{D}{T} \qquad T = \frac{D}{S}$$

○ Density is a measure of how compact an object is. To calculate density, two measurements are needed: mass and volume.

○ Common units of density are: grams per centimetre cubed (g/cm^3) and kilograms per metre cubed (kg/m^3).

A formula triangle can be used to show the connection between mass (M), density (D) and volume (V).

Covering up the quantity required leads to the formulae:

$$M = DV \qquad D = \frac{M}{V} \qquad V = \frac{M}{D}$$

○ Examples of other compound measures are: fuel consumption in kilometres per litre (km/l) and rate of flow in litres per second (l/s).

Example 1 ▷ A train leaves London at 09:30 and arrives in Manchester at 11:54. Find the average speed of the train if the total distance travelled was 180 miles.

Answer 1 T = 2 hours and 24 minutes. Change the minutes to a decimal by dividing the number of minutes by 60: $24 \div 60 = 0.4$, so $T = 2.4$ hours.

$$S = \frac{D}{T} = \frac{180}{2.4} = 75 \text{ mph}$$

Example 2 ▷ A block of wood has a density of 0.8 g/cm^3.

a Find the volume of the block.

b What is the mass of the block?

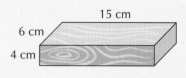

Answer 2 a $V = 15 \times 6 \times 4 = 360 \text{ cm}^3$

b $M = DV = 0.8 \times 360 = 288 \text{ g}$

Exercise 22

1 Beth is taking part in a swimming competition and her time for the 200 m freestyle is 2 minutes and 5 seconds. Calculate her average speed in m/s.

(2 marks)

2 Matthew and Tom travel by road from Town A to Town B along different routes.

Their journey times are the same.

Matthew travels at an average speed of 50 km/h.

Calculate Tom's average speed for the journey. *(2 marks)*

3 On average, John's car uses petrol at the rate of 1 litre for every 15 kilometres travelled.

John drives to a conference at an average speed of 60 km/h and the journey takes him $1\frac{1}{2}$ hours.

Calculate how many litres of petrol he used. *(2 marks)*

4 Sally goes on a five-kilometre walk. The time–distance graph shows her journey.

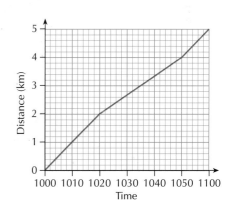

a Between 1000 and 1020, what was her speed in kilometres per hour? *(1 mark)*

b For how many minutes did she travel at this speed on the walk? *(1 mark)*

c At what speed did she start to walk at 1020? *(1 mark)*

5 A train travels between three stations X, Y and Z.

The diagram shows the distances between the stations and the times taken to complete each journey.

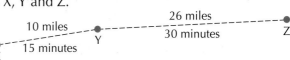

a What is the average speed of the train between X and Y? *(1 mark)*

b What is the average speed of the train between Y and Z? *(1 mark)*

c What is the average speed of the train between X and Z? *(1 mark)*

6 A water tank has a capacity of 5000 litres.

It is filled through a hosepipe, which has a rate of flow of 25 litres per minute.

How long does it take to fill the tank? Give your answer in hours and minutes. *(2 marks)*

Further work on compound measures can be found in Book 9.3 Page 114

23 Angles in a polygon

KEY FACTS

- Polygons are straight-sided shapes such as triangles and quadrilaterals.
- In a regular polygon all sides and angles are the same.
- The sum of the angles in any polygon is always constant. For example, all triangles have an angle sum of 180°, all pentagons have an angle sum of 540°.
- The rule for the angle sum in an n-sided polygon is $(n - 2) \times 180$.
- The exterior angles of all polygons have a sum of 360°.
- The interior angle of a regular n-sided polygon is given by
$$\frac{(n - 2) \times 180}{n}.$$
- The exterior angle of a regular n-sided polygon is given by $\frac{360}{n}$.
- The angles on a straight line add up to 180°.
- The angles at a point add up to 360°.

Example 1 ▷ The diagram shows the side view of a cuboid resting on an isosceles triangle.

Work out the values of the angles a, b and c.

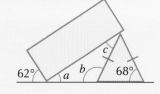

Answer 1
Angle a can be worked out by using angles along a straight line.
$62 + 90 + a = 180$
$a = 180 - 90 - 62 = 28°$

Angle b is the external angle of the isosceles triangle.
$b = 180 - 68 = 112°$

Angle c can be worked out using angles in a triangle.
$c = 180 - 28 - 112 = 40°$

Example 2 ▷ $ABCD$ is a parallelogram.

Calculate the angles p and q.

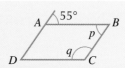

Answer 2
Angle p is an alternate angle to the angle of 55°.
Alternate angles are equal so $p = 55°$.

Angle q is an interior angle between parallel lines with angle p.
Interior angles add up to 180° so $q = 180 - 55 = 125°$.

Exercise 23

1 Work out the values of angles a, b and c in the following diagram.

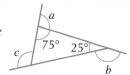

Not to scale

(3 marks)

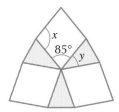

2 The shape on the left has three identical isosceles triangles and three identical rhombi.

Work out the values of the angles x and y. (2 marks)

3 The diagram shows an equilateral triangle.

Work out the values of angles a and b. (2 marks)

4 A quadrilateral can be split into two triangles.

a What is the total of the angles inside a quadrilateral? (1 mark)

b What is the total of the angles inside a hexagon? (1 mark)

5 The diagram shows a parallelogram $ABCD$ inside an isosceles triangle PQR.

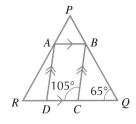

a Angle BQC is 65°. Write down another angle that is 65°. (1 mark)

b Angle BCD is 105°. Write down another angle that is 105°. (1 mark)

c Calculate angle CBQ. (1 mark)

6 The diagram shows a rectangle $PQCD$ inside a regular pentagon $ABCDE$.

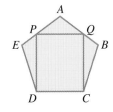

a Write down the value of angle DEP. (1 mark)

b Work out the value of angle QCB. (1 mark)

c Work out the value of angle APQ. (1 mark)

Further work on angles in a polygon can be found in Book 9.1 Pages 55–63
Book 9.2 Pages 52, 56
Book 9.3 Page 73

24 # Pythagoras' theorem

KEY FACTS

○ Pythagoras' theorem states that:

'In a right-angled triangle, the square on the hypotenuse is equal to the sum of the squares on the two smaller sides.'

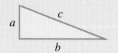

$$c^2 = a^2 + b^2$$

So, where $a = 6$ cm, $b = 8$ cm and $c = 10$ cm, Pythagoras' theorem can be used to prove that this is a right-angled triangle:

$10^2 = 100$ and $6^2 + 8^2 = 36 + 64 = 100$. Hence $c^2 = a^2 + b^2$.

○ Two common right-angled triangles to remember are 3, 4, 5 and 5, 12, 13.

Example 1 ▷ A square of side length 6 cm has been drawn inside a circle.

Calculate the diameter of the circle, giving your answer to 1 decimal place.

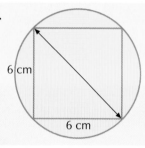

6 cm

6 cm

Answer 1 As the diameter forms part of a right-angled triangle it is possible to use Pythagoras' theorem to calculate its length.

The diameter of the circle will be the hypotenuse of the right-angled triangle. Therefore:

Diameter$^2 = 6^2 + 6^2 = 36 + 36 = 72$

Diameter $= \sqrt{72} = 8.4852814$ cm

The diameter of the circle is therefore 8.5 cm.

Example 2 ▷ A plane flies from Bromby to Leminly.

Leminly is 20 km to the East and 8 km to the North of Bromby.

Calculate the shortest distance from Bromby to Leminly.

Give your answer to three significant figures.

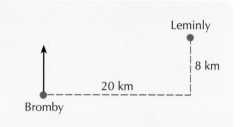

Leminly

8 km

20 km

Bromby

Answer 2 The shortest distance will form a right-angled triangle with the two given distances and it will be the hypotenuse. Therefore:

Distance$^2 = 20^2 + 8^2 = 400 + 64 = 464$

Distance $= \sqrt{464} = 21.540659$

The shortest distance from Bromby to Leminly is 21.5 km.

Exercise 24

 1 Hope is 8.5 km to the East and 4.8 km to the North of Bridgend.

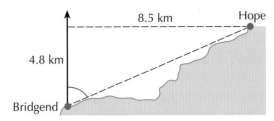

Calculate the direct distance from Bridgend to Hope.

Give your answer to two significant figures. *(3 marks)*

 2 Find the length of the side marked x in this right-angled triangle.

Give your answer to 2 decimal places. *(2 marks)*

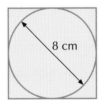

 3 A circle with a diameter of 8 cm is drawn inside a square.

Calculate the length of the square's diagonal, giving your answer to 2 decimal places. *(3 marks)*

 4 Look at the triangle on the right.

Jerry said: 'This is a right-angled triangle'.
Without drawing the triangle, show that Jerry is correct. *(2 marks)*

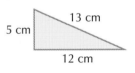

 5 This is Padmini's sketch of all the paths in a park.

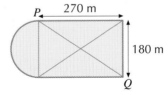

Approximately how long is the diagonal path *PQ*? *(2 marks)*

Further work on Pythagoras can be found in Book 9.3 Page 58

KEY FACTS

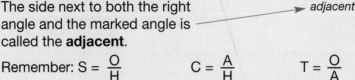

- The longest side of a right-angled triangle is called the **hypotenuse**.
- The side opposite the marked angle is called the **opposite**.
- The side next to both the right angle and the marked angle is called the **adjacent**.

Remember: $S = \dfrac{O}{H}$ $C = \dfrac{A}{H}$ $T = \dfrac{O}{A}$

- Make up a simple sentence to help you remember the above. For example: **S**illy **O**ld **H**arry **C**ould **A**lways **H**ave **T**he **O**ld **A**ttic.
- To start solving a trigonometry problem:
  - i   Identify and draw the right-angled triangle.
  - ii   Put on the given information and mark Hyp, Opp and Adj.
  - iii   Decide which of the sin, cos or tan to use from the above.

Example 1 ▷

A ship is seen as the diagram illustrates.

(The diagram is not drawn to scale.)

Calculate the distance:

a   between the ship and Hellaby lighthouse.

b   from Red Anchor lighthouse to Hellaby lighthouse.

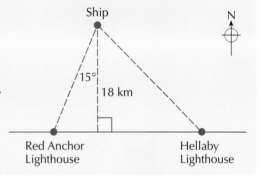

Answer 1

a   X is the distance required on the diagram.
As 65° is the indicated angle, 18 is the opposite.
X is the hypotenuse.

So use $\sin 65 = \dfrac{\text{opposite}}{\text{hypotenuse}} = \dfrac{18}{x}$

so $x = \dfrac{18}{\sin 65} = 19.9$ km.

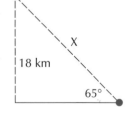

b   The distance required on the diagram is A + B.

To find A: $\tan 15 = \dfrac{\text{opposite}}{\text{hypotenuse}} = \dfrac{A}{x}$

so A = 18 tan15 = 4.82 km.

To find B: $\tan 65 = \dfrac{\text{opposite}}{\text{adjacent}} = \dfrac{18}{B}$

so $B = \dfrac{18}{\tan 65} = 8.39$ km.

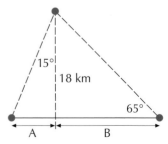

The distance from Red Anchor lighthouse to Hellaby lighthouse is A + B = 4.82 + 8.39 = 13.21 km.

Exercise 25

1 Is it possible to draw a triangle with the measurements shown in the diagram below?

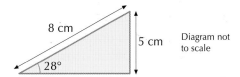

8 cm

5 cm

Diagram not to scale

28°

Use sine, cosine or tangent to explain your answer. *(3 marks)*

2 A table top is in the shape of a trapezium.

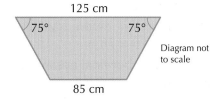

125 cm

75°   75°

Diagram not to scale

85 cm

Calculate the area of the table top. *(3 marks)*

3 A ramp is built to help people get into a doorway.

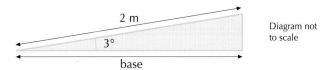

2 m

Diagram not to scale

3°

base

a How long is the base of the ramp? Give your answer to four significant figures. *(3 marks)*

b The recommended slope of a ramp is 1 in 20.

20

1

θ°

Diagram not to scale

What angle, θ, to one decimal place, gives the recommended slope? *(3 marks)*

4 The diagram shows an isosceles triangle. What is the size of the smallest angle in the triangle?

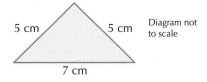

5 cm   5 cm

Diagram not to scale

7 cm

(3 marks)

Further work on trigonometry can be found in Book 9.3 Page 170–180

KEY FACTS

○ The radius is a straight line from the centre of a circle to its circumference. It is equivalent to half of the diameter.

○ The perimeter is a line drawn around the edge of a shape. The circumference is a special name for the perimeter of a circle.

○ Your calculator should have a π button. Always use it. If your calculator does not have a π button use the value 3.142.

○ One formula for the circumference of a circle is $C = \pi d$, where d is the diameter. Another formula is $C = 2\pi r$, where r is the radius.

○ The formula for the area of a circle is $A = \pi r^2$, where r is the radius. Work out r^2 first before multiplying by π. For example, $\pi 5^2 = \pi \times 5^2 = \pi \times 25 = 78.5$.

○ Always ensure that your final answer states the correct units.

Example 1 ▷

a A circle has a radius of 25 cm.

Calculate the area of the circle to 1 decimal place.

b Another circle has a circumference of 150 cm.

Calculate the radius of the circle to 1 decimal place.

25 cm

Answer 1

a Area $= \pi r^2 = \pi \times 25^2 = \pi \times 625 = 1963.5$ cm^2

b If $C = 150$, $2\pi r = 150$

$r = 150 \div 2\pi = 23.9$ cm

Example 2 ▷

A tractor has a front wheel with a diameter of 80 cm and a rear wheel with a diameter of 170 cm.

a What is the circumference of the front wheel?

b The tractor travels 1 kilometre. How many times will the front wheel go round? Give your answer to the nearest 10.

c When the front wheel has turned 100 times, how many times will the rear wheel have turned?

Answer 2

a $C = \pi \times d = \pi \times 80 = 251.3$ cm (1 dp)

b 1 kilometre = 100 000 cm

100 000 $\div$ 251.3 = 397.93 = 400 to the nearest 10

c In 100 turns the front wheel turns $100 \times \pi \times 80 = 25\ 132.7$ cm.

The rear wheel has a circumference of $\pi \times 170 = 534.1$ cm.

25 132.7 $\div$ 534.1 = 47 times

Exercise 26

1 Calculate the perimeter of a semi-circle with a radius of 6 cm. *(2 marks)*

2 A bike has a front wheel with a diameter of 36 cm.

    a What is the circumference of the wheel? *(1 mark)*

    b John rides 10 kilometres. How many times does the wheel turn? Give your answer to the nearest 10. *(2 marks)*

3 Mary has a large circular dining table that has a diameter of 2.5 metres.

For a dinner party each place setting needs a minimum of 75 cm.

Mary wants to invite ten people to dinner. Will she have enough room at the table? Show your working. *(3 marks)*

4 Calculate the area of a semi-circle with a diameter of 20 cm. *(2 marks)*

5 Calculate the shaded area shown.

The inner circle has a radius of 1.2 metres.

The outer circle has a radius of 1.9 metres. *(3 marks)*

6 a A circle has a diameter of 26 cm.
Calculate the circumference of the circle. *(1 mark)*

    b Another circle has an area of 150 cm^2.
Calculate the radius of the circle. *(2 marks)*

7 The diagram shows a circle and a square.

They have the same area.

The square has a side of 5 cm.

What is the diameter of the circle? *(3 marks)*

                                   5 cm

8 The diagram shows a circle and a square.

They have the same perimeter.

The side of the square is 7 cm.

What is the radius of the circle? *(2 marks)*

                                   7 cm

9 The diagram shows a square inside a circle of radius 10 cm.

What percentage of the circle is covered by the square? *(3 marks)*

20 cm

Further work on circumference and area of a circle can be found in Book 9.2 Pages 91, 93
Book 8.3 Pages 77, 79

27 # Circles, sectors and cylinders

LEVEL **8**

KEY FACTS

- The perimeter of a semicircle is $P = \pi r + 2r$ or $P = \frac{1}{2}\pi d + d$.
- The area of a semicircle is $\frac{1}{2}\pi r^2$.
- The volume of a cylinder is $V = \pi r^2 h$, where r is the radius and h is the height.
- The surface area of a cylinder is $A = 2\pi r^2 + 2\pi rh$.
- The area of a sector of a circle with an angle of θ is $\dfrac{\theta}{360} \times \pi r^2$.

Example 1 ▷

A candle is in the shape of a cylinder with a radius of 4 cm and a height of 15 cm.

It burns at the rate of 1 cm per hour.

What is the volume of the candle after it has burnt for $4\frac{1}{2}$ hours?

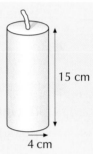

15 cm

4 cm

Answer 1

After $4\frac{1}{2}$ hours the height of the candle will be $10\frac{1}{2}$ cm.

Volume $= \pi \times 4^2 \times 10.5 = 528$ cm³.

Example 2 ▷

A keyring is made from a semicircle of radius 4 cm, a semicircle of radius 2 cm and a cut out circle of radius $\frac{1}{2}$ cm.

Calculate the shaded area.

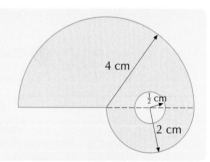

4 cm

$\frac{1}{2}$ cm

2 cm

Answer 2

The area is the sum of a large semicircle with a radius of 4 cm and a small semicircle of radius 2 cm, minus the area of a circle with a radius of $\frac{1}{2}$ cm.

Area $= \frac{1}{2}\pi \times 4^2 + \frac{1}{2}\pi \times 2^2 - \pi \times 0.5^2 = 30.63$ cm².

Exercise 27

1 This shape is made from semicircles.
The diameter of the large semicircle is $6a$.

a Show that the total area of the shape is $3\frac{3}{4}\pi a^2$. *(2 marks)*

b The area of the shape is 12 cm².
Calculate the value of a. Give your answer to one decimal place. *(2 marks)*

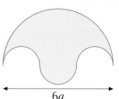

6a

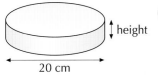

2 What value of r will give the same numerical value for the circumference and the area of a circle? *(2 marks)*

3 A racing car drives around a circular track with a diameter of 2 km.
The car drives at 250 km per hour. How long does it take to complete one circuit of the track? *(2 marks)*

4 A cylinder has a diameter of 20 cm.
The volume of the cylinder is 150π cm³.
What is the height of the cylinder? *(2 marks)*

5 a What fraction of 360 is: **i** 60° **ii** 72°? *(2 marks)*

b The diagram shows two sectors of circles, A and B.

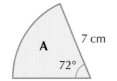 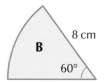

Which sector has the biggest area? *(2 marks)*

c Which sector has the biggest perimeter? *(2 marks)*

d A circle has the same perimeter as that of a semicircle of radius 5 cm.
What is the radius of the small circle?
Give your answer to one decimal place. *(3 marks)*

6 The equator is an imaginary line that passes around the middle of the Earth.
The Earth is approximately a sphere of radius 6400 km.
What is the approximate distance around the equator? *(2 marks)*

7 Cylinder A has a diameter of 12 cm and a height of 5 cm.
Cylinder B has a diameter of 5 cm and a height of 12 cm.
Which cylinder has the greater volume? *(2 marks)*

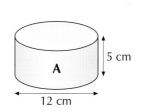 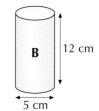

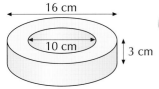

8 A hollow disc has an outside diameter of 16 cm and an inside diameter of 10 cm.
The height of the disc is 3 cm.
Calculate the volume of the disc. *(2 marks)*

9 A sector of a circle of radius 10 cm has an angle of 36°.
Show that the area of the sector is 10π. *(2 marks)*

10 This rectangle and circle have the same area.
What is the radius of the circle? *(2 marks)*

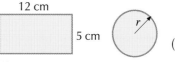

Further work on circles, cylinders and sectors can be found in Book 9.3 Pages 110, 112

(28) Area of plane shapes

KEY FACTS

○ The common metric units for area are mm^2, cm^2 and m^2.
It is useful to learn the following:

$$100 \text{ mm}^2 = 1 \text{ cm}^2 \qquad 10\,000 \text{ cm}^2 = 1 \text{ m}^2$$

○ The formula for the area of a rectangle is:

$$A = lw$$

○ The formula for the area of a triangle is:

$$A = \frac{bh}{2}$$

○ The formula for the area of a parallelogram is:

$$A = bh$$

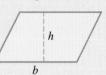

Example 1 ▷ A playground is 20 m long and 30 m wide. What is the area?

Answer 1 Area = lw = 20m × 30m = 600 m^2

Exercise 28

(1) The shapes in this question are drawn on centimetre-square grids.

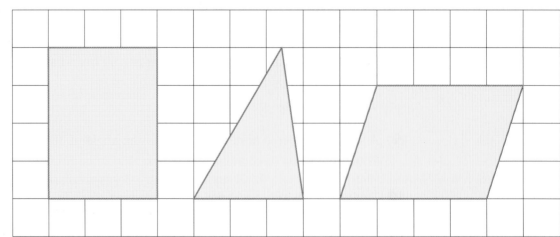

Which of the following statements is true?

A: The rectangle and the parallelogram have the same area.

B: The triangle and the parallelogram have the same area.

C: The rectangle and the triangle have the same area.

D: All the shapes have different areas. *(1 mark)*

2 On a copy of the grid below draw a triangle that has the same area as the parallelogram. *(1 mark)*

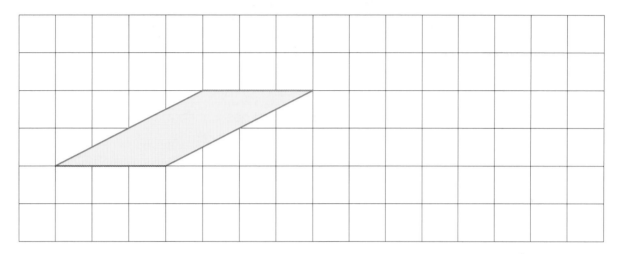

3 Which of the following shapes have an area of 8 cm^2?

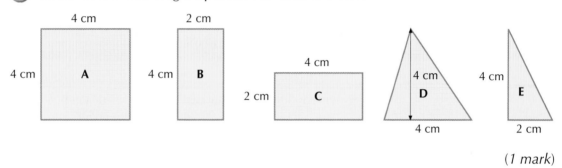

(1 mark)

4 The triangle, square and rectangle below have the same area.

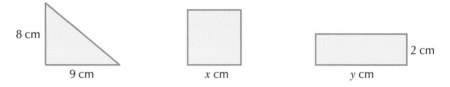

a Work out the value of x. Show your working. *(2 marks)*

b Work out the value of y. Show your working. *(2 marks)*

Further work on areas of plane shapes can be found in

Book 8.1 Pages 63, 65, Book 9.1 Pages 87–92, 183
Book 8.2 Pages 67–73, Book 9.2 Pages 190, 192
Book 9.3 Page 220

29 Volume of 3-D shapes

LEVEL **6, 7**

KEY FACTS

○ The common metric units for volume are mm^3, cm^3 and m^3.
It is useful to learn the following conversions:

$1000\ mm^3$	$= 1\ cm^3$	$1000\ cm^3$	$= 1$ litre
$1\,000\,000\ cm^3$	$= 1\ m^3$	$1\ m^3$	$= 1000$ litres

○ The formula for the volume of a cuboid is:
$$V = lwh$$

○ A prism is a 3-D shape that has a uniform cross-section.
The formula for the volume of a prism is:
$$V = Al$$
where A is the area of the cross-section.

○ The formula for the volume of a cylinder is:
$$V = \pi r^2 l$$
where r is the radius of the circle.

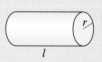

Example 1 ▷ A fish tank has the measurements shown.

a Calculate the volume of the tank.

b How many litres of water can the tank hold when it is full?

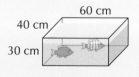

Answer 1 **a** $V = lwh = 60 \times 40 \times 30 = 72\,000\ cm^3$

b $1000\ cm^3 = 1$ litre, so $72\,000 \div 1000 = 72$ litres

Example 2 ▷ A chocolate box is the shape of a triangular prism.

Calculate the volume of the box.

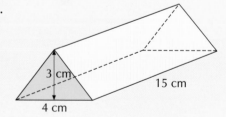

Answer 2 $V = Al$: the area of the triangular cross-section $= \frac{1}{2} \times 4 \times 3 = 6\ cm^2$,
so the volume of the box $= 6 \times 15 = 90\ cm^3$.

Exercise 29

1 Ben has a box of 24 plastic cubes. Each side of a cube measures 1 cm.
He can make only six different cuboids with the cubes.

Copy and complete the table to show the dimensions of these cuboids.

	Dimensions		
Cuboid 1	1	1	24
Cuboid 2	1	2	12
Cuboid 3			
Cuboid 4			
Cuboid 5			
Cuboid 6			

(4 marks)

2 The two cuboids below have the same volume.

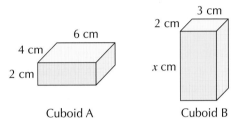

Cuboid A   Cuboid B

a Work out the volume of Cuboid A. *(2 marks)*

b What is the length marked *x* on Cuboid B? *(1 mark)*

3 The diagram on the right shows the dimensions of a swimming pool.

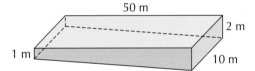

a Calculate the volume of the pool. *(2 marks)*

b How many litres of water are there in the pool when it is full? *(1 mark)*

4 The prisms A and B below have the same cross-sectional area.

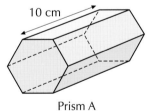
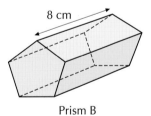

Prism A   Prism B

Find the volume of Prism B, if the volume of Prism A is 400 cm³. *(2 marks)*

5 The internal measurements of a cylindrical tin of dog food are shown on the left.

Calculate the volume of the tin, giving your answer to the nearest cubic centimetre. *(2 marks)*

Further work on volume of 3-D shapes can be found in Book 9.1 Page 93
Book 9.2 Page 97
Book 9.3 Page 112

30 # Congruent and similar shapes

KEY FACTS

o Two shapes are congruent if they are the same size and shape. This means that all the corresponding sides and angles are equal.

o To show that two triangles are congruent, it is sufficient to identify only three corresponding sides or angles. The four cases of congruency are shown below.

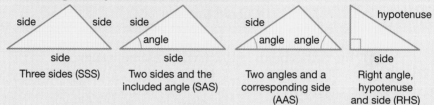

o Two shapes are similar if they are the same shape, but are different in size. This means that all the angles are equal and the corresponding sides are in the same ratio.

o To show that two triangles are similar, the corresponding sides must be in the same ratio.

$$\frac{DE}{AB} = \frac{DF}{AC} = \frac{EF}{BC}$$

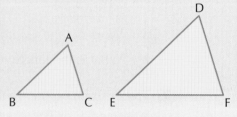

Example 1 ▷ | Explain why these two triangles are congruent.

Answer 1 Two sides are equal and the included angle between the sides is the same.

Example 2 ▷ Triangle ABC is similar to triangle XYZ. Find the side marked x.

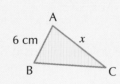

Answer 2 The triangles are similar, so the corresponding sides are in the same ratio.

$$\frac{AC}{XZ} = \frac{AB}{XY} \quad \text{So} \quad \frac{x}{15} = \frac{6}{10} \quad \text{Therefore } x = \frac{90}{10} = 9 \text{ cm}$$

Exercise 30

1 Look at the five triangles below. All the lengths are in centimetres.

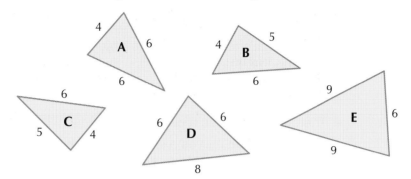

   a   Which two triangles are congruent to each other? Explain why.   (*1 mark*)

   b   Which two triangles are similar to each other but not congruent? Explain why.   (*1 mark*)

2 These two triangles are similar.

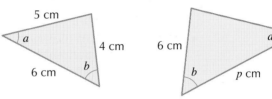

Work out the value of *p*.   (*1 mark*)

3 In the diagram below, triangle ACE is similar to triangle BCD.

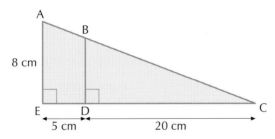

Calculate the length of BD.   (*2 marks*)

4 Below are three tins of different sizes.

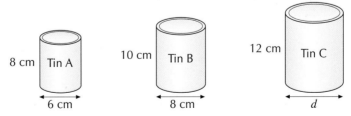

   a   Explain why Tin A is not similar to Tin B.   (*1 mark*)

   b   Tin A is similar to Tin C. Find the diameter, *d*, of Tin C.   (*1 mark*)

Further work on congruent and similar shapes can be found in Book 9.3 Pages 68, 104

Transformations

LEVEL **6, 7, 8**

KEY FACTS

○ A transformation changes the position or size of a shape. The original shape is called the **object** and the transformed shape is the **image**.

○ If the object and image are the same size and shape, the two shapes are said to be **congruent**.

○ There are four basic types of transformation:

- A **translation** moves a shape from one position to another. The object and the image are congruent.
- A **reflection** reflects a shape in a mirror line. The object and the image are congruent. A mirror or tracing paper may be used when doing reflection questions.
- A **rotation** turns a shape through an angle, clockwise or anticlockwise, about a centre of rotation. The object and the image are congruent. Tracing paper may be used when doing rotation questions.
- An **enlargement** makes a shape bigger or smaller about a centre of enlargement by a scale factor. If the scale factor is greater than 1, the image is bigger than the object. If the scale factor is less than 1, the image is smaller than the object. The object and the image are not congruent and the shapes are said to be **similar**.

Example 1 ▶ The rectangle ABCD is shown on the coordinate grid.

Enlarge the rectangle by a scale factor 2 about the origin. Label this rectangle A'B'C'D'.

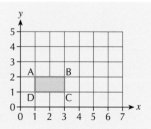

Answer 1

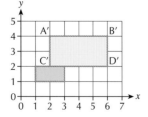

Notice that, since the enlargement is about the origin, the coordinates of the vertices of the object are multiplied by two to give the coordinates of the vertices of the image.

Exercise 31

1 Triangle P is rotated anticlockwise onto triangle Q.

   a On a copy of the diagram, put a cross to mark the centre of rotation.

   b What is the angle of rotation?

   c Reflect triangle P in the mirror line.

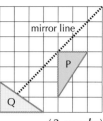

(*3 marks*)

2 On a copy of the coordinate grid, enlarge the triangle by a scale factor 2 about the origin.

(*3 marks*)

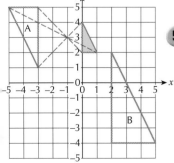

3 Pentagon B is an enlargement of pentagon A with a scale factor $\frac{1}{2}$.

   Write down the values of a, b and c.

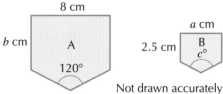

Not drawn accurately

(*3 marks*)

4 The diagram shows a sketch of the equation $y = x^2 - 4$.

Point A is $(0, -4)$. Point B is $(-2, 0)$. Point C is $(2, 0)$.

The curve is reflected in the line $y = 2$.

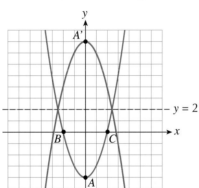

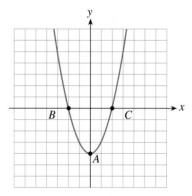

   a What are the coordinates of the image A′ of the point A after the reflection? (*1 mark*)

   b What are the coordinates of the images B′ and C′ of the points B and C after the reflection? (*2 marks*)

5 The diagram shows triangle A which is an enlargement of the shaded triangle by a scale factor −2 about the centre (−1, 3).

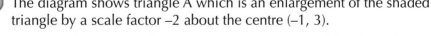

   a Triangle B is an enlargement of scale factor 3 of the shaded triangle. Find the centre of enlargement. (*1 mark*)

   b Draw the position of an enlargement of the shaded triangle with a scale factor of −1 about the centre (−1, 0). (*2 marks*)

Further work on transformations can be found in Book 8.1 Page 104, Book 9.1 Page 138
Book 8.2 Page 107, Book 9.2 Page 140
Book 8.3 Pages 118, 122, Book 9.3 Page 166

32 **Parallel lines**

LEVEL **6**

KEY FACTS

○ Two lines are parallel if they remain the same distance apart.

○ A straight line cutting a pair of parallel lines
is called a **transversal**.

c and e are **alternate** angles (Z angles): they
are equal to each other.

d and f are also **alternate** angles: they equal each other.

d and e are **allied** angles: they add up to 180°.

c and f are also **allied** angles: they add up to 180°.

a and e are **similar** angles, they equal each other.

b and f are also **similar** angles: they equal each other.

Example 1 ▷   The shape on the right is a parallelogram.

Work out the size of angle A.

Give a reason for your answer.

Answer 1   The two marked angles are allied so add up to 180°. Hence $A = 180 – 55 = 125°$.

Example 2 ▷   Mick has drawn a rhombus.

a   Calculate the size of angle d.

b   Calculate the size of angle e.

Answer 2   **a**   The angle marked 65° and angle d are alternate angles so they are equal. Therefore, d is 65°.

b   The angle marked 65° and angle e are allied angles so they add up to 180°. Therefore, e is $180 – 65 = 115°$.

Example 3 ▷   The shape below has two identical white tiles and a triangular tile in between.

a   Calculate the size of angle P.

b   Calculate the size of angle Q.
Show your working.

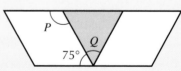

Answer 3   **a** P and the 75° angle are allied angles: $180 – 75 = 105°$ so $P = 105°$.

b $Q = 180 – (2 \times 75) = 30°$

Exercise 32

1 The diagram below shows a triangle drawn between two parallel lines.

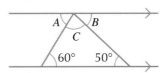

    a Calculate the size of angle *A*.   (*1 mark*)

    b Calculate the size of angle *B*.   (*1 mark*)

    c Calculate the size of angle *C*.   (*1 mark*)

2 Billy drew a parallelogram where the large angle was **three** times the size of the small angle.

    a What is the size of the large angle in terms of *x*?   (*1 mark*)

    b Write down an equation for the sum of the two angles marked on the diagram.   (*1 mark*)

    c Solve this equation to find the size of the small angle.   (*1 mark*)

3 Tim drew the diagram below.

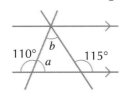

Calculate the size of angle *x*. Explain your answer.   (*2 marks*)

4 Sketch pairs of parallel lines and a transversal showing:

    a a pair of identical allied angles   (*1 mark*)

    b alternate angles of 45°.   (*1 mark*)

5 Look at the following diagram.

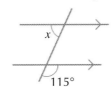

    a Calculate the size of angle *a*.   (*1 mark*)

    b Calculate the size of angle *b*.   (*2 marks*)

Further work on parallel lines can be found in Book 8.2 Page 19
Book 8.3 Page 19

Constructions and loci   LEVEL **7**

KEY FACTS

○ When drawing accurately, you must measure lines to within 1 mm.

○ A locus is the set of all points that fit a given condition or rule. The plural of locus is loci.

○ The locus of a point, which is equidistant from two fixed points A and B, is the perpendicular bisector of the line joining the two points.

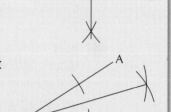

○ The locus of a point, which is equidistant from two fixed lines AB and BC, is the bisector of the angle ABC.

○ Always remember to leave in the construction lines.

Example 1 ▷   Accurately draw a triangle with sides of 5 cm, 6 cm and 8 cm.

Answer 1

Step 1: Draw a base line of 8 cm.

Step 2: Set compasses to 6 cm and draw an arc.

Step 3: Set compasses to 5 cm and draw an arc.

Step 4: Join up the points to complete the triangle.

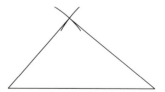

Example 2 ▷   Describe the locus of a point that is always 3 cm from a fixed point **A**.

Answer 2   Set compasses to 3 cm. Draw a circle with its centre at **A**. The locus is a circle of radius 3 cm with its centre at **A**.

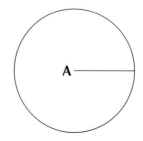

1 Draw this triangle accurately.

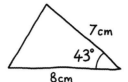

(3 marks)

2 The plan shows the position of three towns A, B and C.

A •

The scale of the plan is 1 cm to 10 km.

A mobile phone mast is to be built.
It needs to be nearer to B than C
and less than 40 km from A.

On a copy of the plan, show the region
where the mast can be built.
Label the region R.

C •

• B

(Remember to leave in your construction lines.)

(3 marks)

3 In this drawing, the shaded area represents a lawn.

A path is to be laid around the lawn so that the edge of the path is always 1 m from the edge of the lawn.

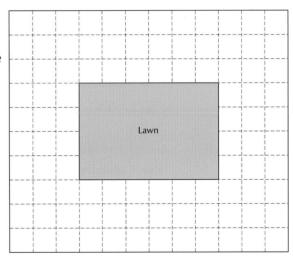

Lawn

Draw a scale drawing to show the position of the path. Use a scale of 1 cm to 1 m.

(2 marks)

4 A goat is tethered by a 3 m length of rope to the corner of a shed that is 1 m by 2 m.

Part of the area that the goat can graze is shown shaded in the diagram.

Draw a scale drawing to show the rest of the area that the goat can graze.

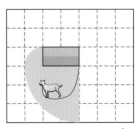

(3 marks)

Further work on loci can be found in Book 9.2 Page 64
Book 9.3 Page 64

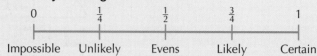
KEY FACTS

○ The probability scale goes from 0 to 1:

0	$\frac{1}{4}$	$\frac{1}{2}$	$\frac{3}{4}$	1
Impossible	Unlikely	Evens	Likely	Certain

○ Probabilities can be written as fractions, decimals or percentages.

○ To calculate the probability of an event, you need to find all the possible outcomes first and then use the formula:

$$P(\text{Event}) = \frac{\text{Number of outcomes for the event}}{\text{Total number of outcomes}}$$

For example, to find P(Even score), when throwing a dice, there are six equally likely outcomes – 1, 2, 3, 4, 5, 6 – and three of these outcomes are even. So P(Even score) = $\frac{3}{6}$ = $\frac{1}{2}$.

○ If the probability of an event happening is p, then the probability of the event not happening is $1 - p$.

○ When two events occur together, the outcomes can be listed or shown in a sample space table.

For example, when two coins are thrown the four outcomes can be listed as: HH, HT, TH, TT or shown in a sample space table:

		First coin	
		H	T
Second coin	H	HH	TH
	T	HT	TT

Example 1 ▷

James and Robert are playing chess.
The probability that James wins the next game is 0.5.
The probability that Robert wins the next game is 0.4.

a What is the probability that the next game is a draw?

b What is the probability that the next game is not a draw?

Answer 1

a P(Draw) = 1 − 0.5 − 0.4 = 0.1   **b** P(Not a draw) = 1 − 0.1 = 0.9

Example 2 ▷

A dice and a coin are thrown together.

a Draw a sample space table to show all the possible outcomes.

b Find the probability that the coin lands on heads and the dice lands on an odd number.

Answer 2

a

		Dice					
		1	2	3	4	5	6
Coin	H	1–H	2–H	3–H	4–H	5–H	6–H
	T	1–T	2–T	3–T	4–T	5–T	6–T

b There are three possible outcomes for a head and odd number: 1–H, 3–H and 5–H. Hence, P(Head and odd) = $\frac{3}{12}$ = $\frac{1}{4}$.

Exercise 34

1 Trevor is playing a game with two fair dice.

The probability that he throws a double six is $\frac{1}{36}$.

   a   What is the probability that he does not throw a double six?

   b   What is the probability that he throws a double two?

   c   What is the probability that he throws any double?   *(3 marks)*

2 Here are two tins of sweets. The sweets are all the same size.

Tin A contains 25 toffees and 15 mints. Tin B contains 28 toffees and 22 mints.

Julie can take a sweet at random from either Tin A or Tin B.

Which tin should she choose to have a better chance of picking a toffee?

Explain your answer.   *(3 marks)*

> The probability that I take out a blue disc is $\frac{1}{4}$ because there is 1 blue disc and 4 red discs in the bag.

3 Beth has four red discs and one blue disc in a bag.

She takes a disc out of the bag without looking in the bag.

Explain why Beth is wrong.   *(1 mark)*

4 This spinner has five equal sections and five numbers are printed on it.

On the spinner, the probability of scoring a 2 is $\frac{1}{5}$ and the probability of scoring an even number is $\frac{3}{5}$.

What numbers could be on the spinner?   *(2 marks)*

5 The following four number cards are placed in a bag.

Marie chooses a card at random, notes its number and then replaces it in the bag.

She takes another card at random and notes its number.

She then adds together the numbers on the two cards she has chosen.

   a   Copy and complete the table to show all the possible outcomes.

First card

+	1	2	3	4
1				
2				
3				
4				

Second card

        (2 marks)

   b   What is the probability that her answer is a multiple of 3?   *(1 mark)*

   c   What is the probability that her answer is not a multiple of 3?   *(1 mark)*

   d   What is the probability that her answer is greater than 10?   *(1 mark)*

Further work on probability can be found in   Book 9.1 Pages 128–135

Book 9.2 Pages 129–136

Book 9.3 Pages 150, 152

35 Relative frequency

KEY FACTS

- If the probability of an event is p, the probability of the event not happening is $1 - p$.
- If the probability of event A is p and the probability of event B is q, the probability of event A or event B occurring is $p + q$.
- Relative frequency, or experimental probability, is the number of successful trials divided by the number of trials altogether.
- The more trials or experiments that are done, the closer the relative frequency gets to the actual (theoretical) probability.

Example 1 ▷ Two fair, six-sided dice are thrown by three students. Their results are shown in the table.

Name	Number of throws	Results		
		No sixes	One 6	Double 6
Alf	20	16	4	0
Beryl	240	164	68	8
Chas	100	65	30	5

a Which student's data is most likely to give the best estimate of the true probability of throwing no sixes, one 6 and double 6? Explain your answer.

b The results are pooled together.

Number of throws		Results		
		No sixes	One 6	Double 6
360		245	102	13

Use the combined results to estimate the probability of throwing:
  i No sixes **ii** One 6 **iii** A double 6 with two dice.

c The theoretical probability of each result is:

P(no sixes) = $\frac{25}{36}$ P(one 6) = $\frac{10}{36}$ P(double 6) = $\frac{1}{36}$

Use these probabilities to work out how many of each result you would expect from 360 throws.

d Explain why the students' results are not the same as the theoretical results.

Answer 1

a Beryl as she has had the most throws.

b **i** $\frac{245}{360}$ or 0.68   **ii** $\frac{102}{360}$ or 0.28   **iii** $\frac{13}{360}$ or 0.04

c 250 with no 6, 100 with one 6 and 10 double sixes.

d The students' results are from a real experiment, so there is an element of chance.

Example 2 ▶

A bag contains only blue, green and red balls. There are 40 balls in the bag altogether. The probability of picking a blue ball at random from the bag is $\frac{2}{5}$.

   a   What is the probability of taking a ball that is not blue from the bag?

   b   What is the greatest number of red balls that could be in the bag?

Answer 2

   a   The probability of a blue ball is $\frac{2}{5}$ so P(not blue) = $1 - \frac{2}{5} = \frac{3}{5}$.

   b   There are 16 blue balls ($\frac{2}{5} \times 40$). There must be at least one green ball so the most red balls there could be is 23.

Exercise 35

1 The probability of taking an orange sweet from a bag of sweets is $\frac{1}{8}$.

    What is the probability of taking a sweet from the bag that is **not** orange?   *(1 mark)*

2 Packets of football cards contain pictures of European footballers.

   a   The probability of a picture being of a player in the English league is 0.3. Tom buys 40 cards. How many English league players should he expect to have?   *(1 mark)*

   b   Sandra buys some cards and gets 16 pictures of players in the Spanish league. She estimates that the probability of getting a Spanish league player is 0.4. How many cards did she buy?   *(2 marks)*

   c   The makers of the cards claim that the probability of getting a player in the Italian League is 0.2. Eric buys ten cards and gets three Italian league players. Is the manufacturer's claim correct? Explain your answer.   *(1 mark)*

3 A group of lower school students have volunteered for a job. The table shows the probability of selecting one of the students at random.

Year	Boy	Girl
Year 7	0.15	0.2
Year 8	0.1	0.25
Year 9	0.05	0.25

   a   One student is selected at random. What is the probability that the student will be:

      i a boy?   **ii** **not** in Year 7?   *(2 marks)*

   b   60 students volunteer altogether. How many of them are Year 7 boys?   *(1 mark)*

   c   The student selected is in Year 9. Is the student more likely to be a boy or a girl? Explain your answer.   *(1 mark)*

Further work on probability and relative frequency can be found in Book 9.2 Page 134

Book 9.3 Page 157

36 Probability of combined events

KEY FACTS

○ Combined events are two independent events, such as throwing a dice and tossing a coin, which follow each other.

○ The probability of event A followed by event B is P(A) × P(B).

○ There are usually two ways that event A and event B can occur together:

P(event A and event B) = P(A followed by B) or P(B followed by A).

This is worked out as P(A and B) = P(A) × P(B) + P(B) × P(A).

○ The probability of the same event occurring twice is P(A) × P(A).

○ The probability of an event occurring just once in two trials is P(A) × P(A') + P(A') × P(A), where A' represents the event 'Not A'.

Example 1 ▷

When Mr Jones drives to work he passes two sets of lights.

He knows that the probability he will be stopped at the first set of lights is 0.3, and that the probability he will be stopped at the second set of lights is 0.8.

a What is the probability that Mr Jones will have to stop at both sets of lights?

b What is the probability that he will have to stop at only one set of lights?

c Mr Jones drives to work 200 times a year. Estimate how many times he will drive through both sets of lights without stopping.

Answer 1

a P(stops at both sets) = P(stops at first set) × P(stops at second set)
= 0.3 × 0.8 = 0.24

b P(stops at only one set) = P(stops at first set and not at second set) + P(does not stop at first set and stops at second) = 0.3 × 0.2 + 0.7 × 0.8
= 0.06 + 0.56 = 0.62

c P(does not stop) = 0.7 × 0.2 = 0.14
In 200 journeys he will not be stopped on 200 × 0.14 = 28 times.

Example 2 ▷

A mouse is placed in the maze shown at point S.

At each junction the mouse has an equal chance of taking either path.

a There are two ways that the mouse can get from S to mouse hole B. Draw these two routes on the diagram.

b What is the probability that the mouse ends up in mouse hole A?

c What is the probability that the mouse ends up in mouse hole B?

Answer 2   **a**

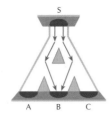

b   To get to mouse hole A, the mouse has to make two choices to go right at each junction.
P(right and right) = P(right) × P(right) = $\frac{1}{2}$ × $\frac{1}{2}$ = $\frac{1}{4}$

c   To get to mouse hole B the mouse has to go right then left or left then right.
P(L then R) or P(R then L) = P(L) × P(R) + P(R) × P(L) = $\frac{1}{2}$ × $\frac{1}{2}$ + $\frac{1}{2}$ × $\frac{1}{2}$ = $\frac{1}{4}$ + $\frac{1}{4}$ = $\frac{1}{2}$

Exercise 36

1   Two bags contain red and blue balls. Bag A has 12 red and 8 blue balls.
Bag B has 10 red and 6 blue balls. I can choose a ball from either bag.
I want to choose a red ball. Which bag should I choose?   *(2 marks)*

2   A company makes widgets. The company knows that the probability that any widget will be defective is $\frac{1}{20}$.

    a   A box contains 4000 widgets. How many of the widgets are likely to be defective?   *(1 mark)*

    b   Two widgets are tested at random. Calculate the probability that both widgets are defective.   *(2 marks)*

    c   Calculate the probability that only one of the widgets will be defective.   *(2 marks)*

3   When a coin is thrown once it can land two ways: a head (H) or a tail (T).
When a coin is thrown twice it can land four ways: HH, HT, TH, TT.

    a   When a coin is thrown three times it can land eight ways. Three of these are HHH, HHT and HTH. List the other five ways the coin can land.   *(1 mark)*

    b   Explain why the probability of getting two heads when a coin is thrown twice is $\frac{1}{4}$.   *(1 mark)*

    c   What is the probability of getting one head and one tail when a coin is thrown twice?   *(1 mark)*

    d   What is the probability of getting three heads when a coin is thrown three times?   *(1 mark)*

4   **a**   A fair dice is thrown once. What is the probability of scoring:
       i   6   **ii**   Any other value than 6.   *(2 marks)*

    b   A game costs £1 a go. A fair dice is thrown twice.
       If the dice lands on a 6 twice then the player wins £10. If it lands on a 6 once in the two throws the player gets their £1 back. If no 6 is thrown in either go the player loses their money.
       i   Show that the probability of getting your money back is $\frac{10}{36}$.   *(2 marks)*
       ii   What is the probability of winning £10?   *(1 mark)*
       iii   Simon has 36 goes. How much can he expect to win or lose?   *(2 marks)*

Further work on the probability of combined events can be found in Book 9.3 Page 155

Surveys and questionnaires

KEY FACTS

- When a survey is carried out it should give reliable and unbiased data.
- The sample size should be big enough to give reliable results (at least 30).
- The sample should be representative and not just taken from one type of person or a group of friends.
- The sample should be chosen in such a way that it gives a representative sample, e.g. random sampling, quota sampling.
- Questions on questionnaires should **not**:
  - ask for more than one thing at a time
  - be offensive
  - be worded in a way that forces people to answer in a particular way
  - ask things that might embarrass the person being surveyed.
- Responses on questionnaires should:
  - cover all possible responses
  - give ranges for things like age and income
  - not have any overlapping boxes
  - be kept to a reasonable number (six maximum).

Example 1 ▷ A class decides to find out if students in their school would like a new uniform.

a Jasmin says: 'I will ask ten of my friends what they want.'
Give two reasons why Jasmin's method might not produce good data.

b Davos decides to use a questionnaire. This is one of his questions:
The school uniform is very ugly and not very practical. Don't you agree?
☐ Agree a lot   ☐ Agree a little

Give two reasons why Davos' question is not a good one.

c Tamsin says: 'I will send 100 questionnaires around school.'
Which one of the following methods will give the most reliable data?
A: Asking 100 Year 11 students.
B: Asking the first 100 students on the school register.
C: Putting all the names of students in a hat and drawing out 100 names to ask.

Answer 1 **a** The sample size is too small to give reliable results. Also, asking a group of friends is not likely to give unbiased data as the sample is not representative.

b The question is a leading question as it gives Davos' opinion. It is also badly written as there are two questions in one.

The reponse section only gives options where you have to agree. There is no box to tick if you disagree.

c Method C will give the most reliable data as it is random so gives everyone an equal chance of being picked. Method A would not be representative. Method B may give a good spread of views but is not random.

Exercise 37

1 Some students decide to carry out a survey to find out if people like a new rap artist.

a One question was: How old are you?

☐ 10 or younger ☐ 10 to 15 ☐ 15 to 20 ☐ Over 20

Marita said: *The labels for the middle two boxes need changing*

Explain why Marita is right. *(1 mark)*

b Another question was:

How much do you spend on CDs each month?

☐ Nothing ☐ A bit ☐ A lot ☐ Don't know

Marita said some of the labels also need changing.
Write new labels for some or all of the boxes. *(2 marks)*

c The students decide to survey 100 people.
Devon decides to ask 100 students in school.

i Give one disadvantage of this suggestion. *(1 mark)*

ii Give one advantage of this suggestion. *(1 mark)*

2 These are two questions on Billy's survey on shopping habits.

Question 1 How much do you spend each week on groceries?

☐ £20 or less ☐ £21 to £30 ☐ £31 to £40 ☐ £41 to £50 ☐ Over £50

Give one reason why this is a good question. *(1 mark)*

Question 2 How many times a week do you buy fruit and/or vegetables?

☐ None ☐ 1 or 2 ☐ 3 ☐ 4 or more ☐ Every day

Give one reason why this is not a good question. *(1 mark)*

3 Karen and Darren want to conduct a survey to find out students' favourite school subjects.

a Karen decides to survey the 34 students in her Maths class.

i Give one disadvantage of Karen's method. *(1 mark)*

ii Give one advantage of Karen's method. *(1 mark)*

b Darren decides to ask the 15 members of the school football team.
Give two disadvantages of Darren's method. *(2 marks)*

Further work on surveys and questionnaires can be found in Book 9.1 Page 176
Book 9.2 Page 183
Book 9.3 Page 212

38 Discrete and grouped data

KEY FACTS

○ Discrete data is data that can take individual values.

○ Continuous data is data that can take any value in a range of values.

○ Discrete frequency tables are a convenient way of recording large data sets of discrete data where much of the data has the same values.

○ Grouped frequency tables are a convenient way of recording large data sets of continuous data by grouping the data together.

○ Frequency polygons are used to show the shape of distributions and to compare distributions. The mid-point of the group is plotted against the frequency.

Example 1 ▷

Some field mice were caught and weighed in October.

The masses are given to the nearest gram.

The results are shown in the table.

Mass of each mouse (grams)	Frequency f	Mid-point of group m	$m \times f$
16–20	13	18	234
21–25	20	23	
26–30	31		
31–35	17		
36–40	4		

a How many field mice were weighed altogether?

b Calculate an estimate of the mean weight of the field mice.
You may complete the table to help you.
Give your answer to 1 decimal place.

c Field mice with a mass of 22 grams or less will not survive the winter.
Estimate how many of the mice surveyed will not survive the winter.

d Draw a frequency polygon to show the distribution of masses of the mice.

e Explain why it is not possible to find the range of the masses of the field mice.

Answer 1

a 85. Add up the total frequency.

b 26.8 (1 dp). The missing mid-points are 28, 33 and 38.
Complete the $m \times f$ column: 460, 868, 561, 152.
The total $m \times f$ is 2275.
The mean is $2275 \div 85 = 26.7647$.

c 21. There are 20 mice in the group 21–25 so there
will be approximately 8 with masses of 21 and
22 grams. Add this to the 13 in the first group.

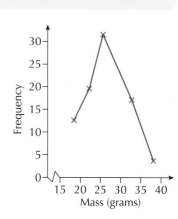

d Plot the frequencies against the mid-points of the group: (18, 13), (23, 20), (28, 31) etc as shown on the previous page.

e There is no indication of the actual masses of the mice, only the group they are in.

Exercise 38

1 Sandra has 12 bags of marbles. The mean number of marbles per bag is 36.

Number of marbles in a bag	34	35	36	37	38
Frequency	3	2	1	4	1

The table shows how many marbles are in 11 of the bags.
Calculate how many marbles are in the twelfth bag. *(3 marks)*

2 A survey was done of birds' nests in a small wood.

Number of eggs found in nest	1	2	3	4	5
Frequency	13	23	16	5	4

61 nests were surveyed and the number of eggs in each was counted.

a Show that the total number of eggs found was 147. *(1 mark)*

b Calculate the mean number of eggs per nest.
Give your answer to 1 decimal place. *(2 marks)*

c It is known that 80% of eggs hatch.
In another large wood there are known to be 526 nests.
Estimate the number of eggs in the large wood that will hatch.
Give your answer to the nearest 10. *(2 marks)*

3 The table shows the heights of 100 tulips grown in a greenhouse.

Height of tulip h (cms)	Frequency f	Mid-point of group m	$m \times f$
$25 < h \le 30$	11	27.5	302.5
$30 < h \le 35$	23	32.5	
$35 < h \le 40$	31		
$40 < h \le 45$	19		
$45 < h \le 50$	16		
Total	100		

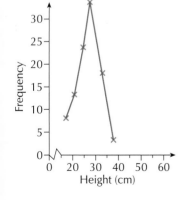

a Calculate an estimate of the mean height of a tulip. Copy and complete the table to help you. *(2 marks)*

b The frequency polygon on the left shows the distribution of the heights of 100 tulips grown outside. On a copy of the same graph, draw the frequency polygon for the heights of the tulips grown in a greenhouse. *(1 mark)*

c Will the mean height of the tulips grown outside be greater or smaller than the mean of the tulips grown in the greenhouse?
Explain your answer. *(1 mark)*

Further work on grouped data and frequency diagrams can be found in Book 9.3 Page 95

39 **Pie charts**

KEY FACTS

○ The sectors in a pie chart represent the proportions, not the numbers, so be careful when comparing two pie charts.

○ The angles of the sectors in the pie chart all add up to 360°.

○ Remember the common percentages in pie charts:
   50% will be a semi-circle sector
   25% will be a quarter of a circle, right-angled sector.

○ If asked to sketch a pie chart, do remember to correctly label each sector.

Example 1 ▷

The following pie charts show information about the ages of people in two areas of Sheffton. There are 8 thousand people in Grimthorpe, and 2.5 thousand people in Tutly.

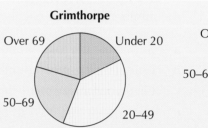

Grimthorpe

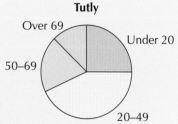

Tutly

a About what percentage of people in Grimthorpe are aged 50–69?

b Jess says:

The pie charts show that there are more people under 20 in Tutly than in Grimthorpe.

Jess is wrong.
Explain why the charts do not show this.

c There are about 50 thousand people in Sheffton.

The table shows the approximate percentages of the people in Sheffton in the various age groups.

Under 20	20–49	50–69	Over 69
25%	40%	20%	15%

Sketch a pie chart to show the information in the table.

Label each section clearly with the age group.

Answer 1

a 25%. The sector is a right angle, indicating about one quarter of the people in Grimthorpe are in the age group 50–69.

b Because there are more than three times as many people in Grimthorpe than Tutly, the actual number of people under 20 will be much bigger in Grimthorpe.

c

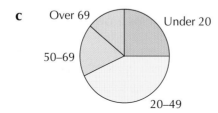

Exercise 39

1 100 members of Avery Youth Club were asked the question: 'Would you play table tennis?'

The pie chart on the right shows their answers.

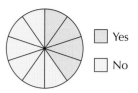

a How many of the youth club members would not play table tennis? *(1 mark)*

b In Banner Cross Youth Club, 50 members were asked the same question.

60% of these members said they would play table tennis.

Which one of the following three pie charts below illustrates this? *(1 mark)*

i 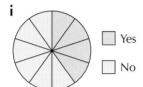 **ii** 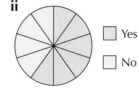 **iii**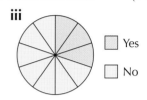

Banner Cross Youth Club
50 members

c How many members of Banner Cross Youth Club said that they would play table tennis? *(1 mark)*

d Emily compares the pie charts and says: 'More members in Banner Cross Youth Club said they would play table tennis than in Avery Youth Club.'

Explain why Emily is wrong. *(1 mark)*

2 Henry paid £540 in council tax one year.
The table shows how the money was spent by the council.
Sketch a pie chart to show the council's spending. *(2 marks)*

Service	Amount
Education	£243
Health	£81
Social Services	£108
Other	£108
Total	£540

3 The following pie chart shows the favourite pets of a number of students.

The angle for 'Cat' is 72°, which represents nine students.

a How many students were surveyed altogether? *(1 mark)*

b 13 students chose 'Dog'. What angle would represent 'Dog'? *(1 mark)*

c In drawing the chart Suzie drew the angle for 'Rabbit' as 90°. Explain why this is not possible. *(1 mark)*

Favourite pets of students

Further work on pie charts can be found in Book 8.1 Page 131
Book 8.2 Page 138
Book 8.3 Page 151

40 Scatter diagrams and lines of best fit LEVEL 6, 7

KEY FACTS

- Scatter diagrams show the relationship between two variables.
- The relationship between the variables is called correlation.
- The following diagrams show the main types of correlation.

Strong positive   Weak positive   No correlation   Weak negative   Strong negative

- A line of best fit should be drawn to pass through the middle of the data and be as close to as many points as possible.
- The line of best fit can be used to predict the value of one variable from the value of the other variable.
- When using a line of best fit always draw lines from the axes to show how values were found.
- Lines of best fit do not have to go through the origin.
- Correlation is only valid over the range of the data. Beyond this it is not possible to say if the relationship is valid.

Example 1

Flowers open their petals during the day as they warm up in the sun.

The scatter diagram shows the diameter of the petals at different times of day for a certain flower. The line of best fit is also drawn.

a Estimate the diameter of a flower at 10 AM.

b Estimate by how may centimetres per hour the petals are expanding.

c Explain why you cannot use the scatter diagram to estimate the diameter of the flower at 6 PM.

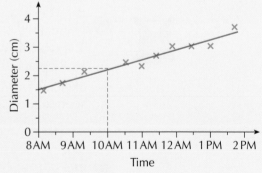

Answer 1

a Draw a line from 10 AM on the Time axis up to the line of best fit, then draw a line across to the vertical axis (dotted on the diagram). This gives a diameter of 2.25 cm.

b At 8 AM the diameter is 1.5 cm and at 2 PM the diameter is 3.5 cm.
So in four hours the increase in diameter is 2 cm. This is 0.5 centimetres per hour.

c The graph only shows the increase from 8 AM to 2 PM. There is no reason to suspect that it continues past this time. In fact, the sun could go in and as it cools down the diameter of the petals will decrease.

Exercise 40

1 The two scatter diagrams below show information about some shops.

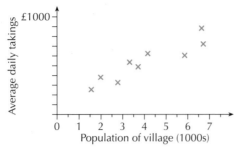 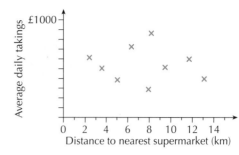

a What does the first graph tell you about the relationship between average daily takings and the population of the village? *(1 mark)*

b What does the second graph tell you about the relationship between average daily takings and the distance to the nearest supermarket? *(1 mark)*

c Draw a line of best fit on the first graph. *(1 mark)*

d A shop opens in a village with a population of 5000 people. What are the expected average daily takings? *(1 mark)*

2 The scatter diagram on the left shows the average daily hours of sunshine and the average daily rainfall for ten towns in August.

a Describe the relationship shown by the scatter diagram. *(1 mark)*

b Copy the graph and draw a line of best fit through the data. *(1 mark)*

c Another town has a daily average rainfall of 0.5 cm. Estimate the average daily hours of sunshine for that town. *(1 mark)*

d A third town has a daily average rainfall of 3 cm. Explain why you cannot use the scatter diagram to estimate the average daily hours of sunshine. *(1 mark)*

3 The scatter diagrams show the test results of 15 students in English, Maths and Science.

The following scatter diagrams show the results.

a Which of these statements most closely describes the relationship between the scores in the tests. *(2 marks)*

Maths and Science

| Strong negative correlation | Weak negative correlation | No correlation | Weak positive correlation | Strong positive correlation |

Maths and English

| Strong negative correlation | Weak negative correlation | No correlation | Weak positive correlation | Strong positive correlation |

b Which statement most closely describes the relationship between the scores in Science and English. *(1 mark)*

Science and English

| Strong negative correlation | Weak negative correlation | No correlation | Weak positive correlation | Strong positive correlation |

Further work on scatter diagrams and lines of best fit can be found in Book 9.2 Page 74
Book 9.3 Pages 82 and 85

41 Median and mean

KEY FACTS

○ The median is the middle value when the data is written in order (or the average of the middle two numbers).

○ To calculate a mean, sum all the values and then divide by the number of items of data.

Example 1 ▷ Find the median and mean of the following set of data:

19, 24, 24, 18, 22, 24, 27, 18.

Answer 1 Sort the data into order, smallest first: 18, 18, 19, 22, 24, 24, 24, 27.

To calculate the median, we must take the average of the two middle numbers as there are eight numbers in the set.

Therefore, the median $= \dfrac{22 + 24}{2} = 23$

To calculate the mean, add together all the numbers and divide by 8.

Therefore, the mean $= \dfrac{18 + 18 + 19 + 22 + 24 + 24 + 24 + 27}{8} = 22$

Example 2 ▷ Nails are packed into boxes. The table shows the number of nails in 20 boxes.

Number of nails in a box	50	51	52	53	54	55
Frequency	7	5	0	2	5	1

a Show that the total number of nails is 1036.

b Calculate the mean number of nails in each box.

c In ten other boxes the mean number of nails in each box is 53.0. Calculate the mean number of nails in all 30 boxes.

Answer 2 a The total number of nails $= (7 \times 50) + (5 \times 51) + (2 \times 53) + (5 \times 54) + (1 \times 55)$
$= 350 + 255 + 106 + 270 + 55 = 1036$. Therefore, there are 1036 nails in total.

b There are 20 boxes. Therefore the mean $= \dfrac{1036}{20} = 51.8$ nails.

c The total number of nails in the 10 boxes $= 53.0 \times 10 = 530$ nails.
The total number of nails in the 30 boxes $= 1036 + 530 = 1566$.

Therefore, the mean number of nails in all 30 boxes $= \dfrac{1566}{30} = 52.2$ nails.

Exercise 41

1 In a game three points are awarded for a win, one point for a draw and no points for losing.

   a Onur played ten games. He won five games, drew three and lost the other two.

      What was Onur's mean score over the ten games? *(1 mark)*

   b George also played ten games. His mean score was 2.3 points.

      Copy and complete the table of results for George.

Number of games won	
Number of games drawn	
Number of games lost	

(1 mark)

2 Look at the four cards below. Three expressions are shown. One is hidden.

       $2x + 4$ **?** $2x$ $2x - 3$

   The **mean** value of the expressions is $2x$. What is the hidden expression? *(1 mark)*

3 This table shows the number of peas in 30 pods.

Number of peas in pod	1	2	3	4	5
Frequency	1	6	9	11	3

   a Show that the **total** number of peas in the pods is 99. *(1 mark)*

   b Explain why the **mean** number of peas is 3.3. *(1 mark)*

   c A restaurant serves an average of 35 peas with each meal. They serve 1000 peas on one evening. Approximately how many meals do they serve? *(2 marks)*

4 A school sells bottles of water. Over ten days, the mean number of bottles sold each day is 83.

The table shows the sales of bottles of water over the first eight days.

Number of bottles of water sold	80	81	82	83	84	85
Frequency	3	1	0	2	0	2

Calculate the number of bottles of water sold on the last two days. *(2 marks)*

5 The table shows some of the ages of 20 people.

   a Copy and complete the table. *(1 mark)*

Age group (years)	0–9	10–19	20–29
Mid value (x)	5		
Frequency (f)	2	7	

   b Matt says that the median age of the 20 people is 15 years. Is he correct? Explain your answer. *(1 mark)*

   c Calculate an estimate of the mean age using the mid values. *(2 marks)*

Further work on median and mean can be found in Book 9.1 Page 178
Book 9.2 Page 185
Book 9.3 Page 215, 95

KEY FACTS

○ A stem-and-leaf diagram is a way of showing ordered data in a concise way.

○ The stem will normally be the tens digit and the leaves will be the units digit of a number.

○ All stem-and-leaf diagrams should have a key.

○ Always check the key to make sure what values are being represented.

○ Box plots are a way of showing the essential values for sets of discrete and continuous data.

○ There are five main values on a box plot.

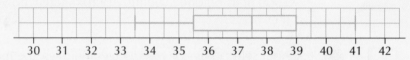

smallest value   Lower quartile   Median   Upper quartile   Largest value

○ The difference between the upper and lower quartiles is known as the interquartile range.

Example 1 ▷ The box plot shows the heights of daffodils grown in a greenhouse.

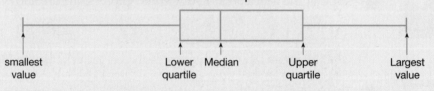

30 31 32 33 34 35 36 37 38 39 40 41 42

Below is some data about the heights of daffodils grown in the garden.

Lowest value	Lower quartile	Median	Upper quartile	Highest value
30.5 cm	33 cm	36 cm	37.5 cm	39 cm

a On the same diagram draw the box plot for the heights of the daffodils grown outside.

b Comment on the difference in average height of the daffodils grown inside compared to those grown outside.

c Comment on the difference in the consistency of the height of the daffodils grown inside and those grown outside.

Answer 1   **a**

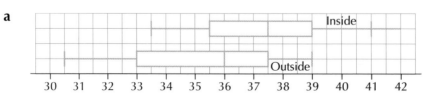

30 31 32 33 34 35 36 37 38 39 40 41 42

b The median height of the daffodils grown inside is 1.5 cm higher than the daffodils grown outside.

c The daffodils grown inside have an interquartile range of 3.5 cm which is more consistent than that of the daffodils grown outside which is 4.5 cm.

Exercise 42

1 The stem-and-leaf diagram below shows how many driving lessons a number of learner drivers had before they took their driving test.

```
0 | 9
1 | 3   4   4   7   8
2 | 4   5   5   5   6   8   9
3 | 2   5   8
4 | 6   9
```

Key
| 2 | 4 represents 24 lessons

a How many learner drivers took part in the survey? *(1 mark)*

b What was the least number of lessons taken? *(1 mark)*

c What was the range of the number of lessons taken? *(1 mark)*

d What was the modal number of lessons taken? *(1 mark)*

e What is the median number of lessons taken? *(1 mark)*

f Half of the learners who took less than 20 lessons failed their test.

A quarter of the learners who took more than 20 lessons failed their test.

How many of the learner drivers failed their test? *(1 mark)*

2 The box plot shows the times taken by a group of girls to run 100 metres.

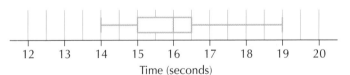

The times taken by a group of boys to run 100 metres was also recorded.

- The slowest boy took the same time as the slowest girl.
- The range of the boys' times was 2 seconds greater than the girls' range.
- The median of the boys' times was the same as the lower quartile of the girls' times.
- The boys' interquartile range was the same as the girls' interquartile range.

Draw a box plot for the boys' times. *(3 marks)*

3 The two box plots show the weights of a bat colony measured in May and October.

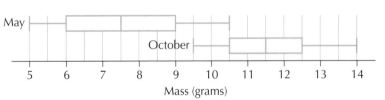

a What is the difference in the median weights? *(1 mark)*

b In which month is the interquartile range the greatest, and by how much? *(1 mark)*

c The two distributions of weights are different. Give a reason why. *(1 mark)*

Further work on stem-and-leaf diagrams and box plots can be found in Book 8.1 Page 129
Book 8.2 Page 136
Book 8.3 Page 148

KEY FACTS

○ Cumulative frequency means to accumulate or build up frequency.

○ Cumulative frequency diagrams can use either straight lines or curves.

○ Important information can be read off from the horizontal axis of the graph:
  - the median
  - the lower quartile
  - upper quartile.

○ The interquartile range, a measure of spread, is the difference between the lower and upper quartiles.

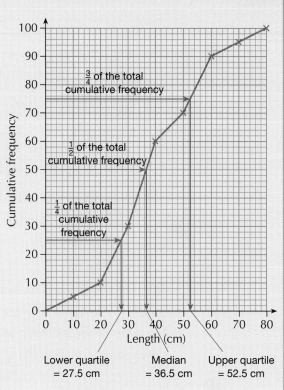

Lower quartile = 27.5 cm   Median = 36.5 cm   Upper quartile = 52.5 cm

Interquartile range = Upper quartile – Lower quartile.

Example 1 ▷ The cumulative frequency diagram above shows information about the lengths of 100 pieces of wood.

This table provides some information about the lengths of 100 pieces of metal.

Compare the lengths of wood and the lengths of metal.

Lower quartile	30 cm
Median	40 cm
Upper quartile	**50 cm**

Answer 1 Compare the medians: The median for wood = 36.5 cm; the median for metal = 40 cm.

This means that on average the lengths of wood are shorter than the lengths of metal.

Compare the interquartile range:

The interquartile range for wood = 52.5 cm – 27.5 cm = 25 cm;
The interquartile range for metal = 52.5 cm – 27.5 cm = 25 cm.

Therefore the lengths of the pieces of metal are less spread out or more consistent.

Exercise 43

1 Lee carried out a survey into the amount of time people spent at a museum. She asked 80 people. The cumulative frequency diagram below shows her results.

a Use the graph to estimate the median number of hours at the museum. *(1 mark)*

b Use the graph to estimate the interquartile range of the number of hours at the museum. *(2 marks)*

c Scott carried out a similar survey at a theme park. This is what he found:

The median number of hours was 3.4 hours; the interquartile range was 1.1 hours.

Compare the number of hours spent at the museum and at the theme park.

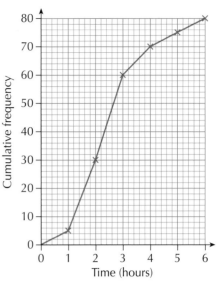

2 A student recorded the heights of boys in his class. He summarised the results, then drew a box plot.

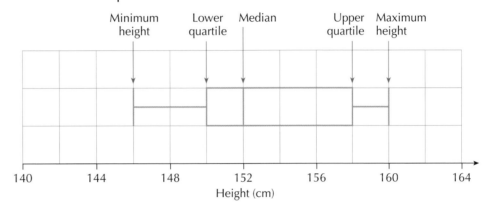

He then recorded the heights of girls in his class.

He summarised the results, then drew a cumulative frequency diagram.

Compare the heights of boys and girls. *(3 marks)*

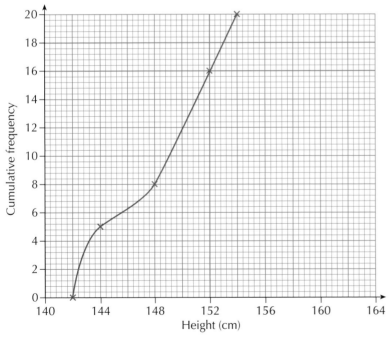

Further work on cumulative frequency can be found in Book 9.3 Pages 93, 217

Answers

Exercise 1 Significant figures, approximation

1 **a** **i** 45 g   **ii** 54.999 recurring g   **b** 8×45 g = 360 g
2 An explanation saying that some of the seven numbers must have been rounded down. Hence their sum is less than 100.
3 **a** $200 \times 500 \div 20 = 5000$
   b $800 \times 100 \div 2 = 40\,000$
4 **a** 12   **b** 15   **c** 8   **d** Any answer between 10 and 15
5 **a** 4.559924598   **b** 4.6

Exercise 2 Negative numbers

1 **a** $-3, -15$ **b** $-10, -4$
2 **a** Any valid values e.g. -2×-10, -1×-20, -4×-5
   b Any valid values e.g. $-4 - -24$, $-8 - -28$,
3 **a** 4, -3 (1 mark for any two values with a product of -12, 1 mark for any two values which add together to make 1)
   b $-2, -6$ (1 mark for any two numbers with a product of 12, 1 mark for any two numbers which add together to make -8)
   c -6
4 **a** -2 **b** -15 **c** -8 **d** -16 **e** $+8$ **f** -10
5 **a** $+7$ **b** $-7, -12$ **c** $+7, +12$ **d** $+7, -7$

Exercise 3 Fractions

1 **a** $1\frac{1}{3}$ cm^2 (1 mark for $\frac{1}{2} \times \frac{4}{5} \times \frac{10}{3}$, 1 mark for units)
   b 30 (1 mark if method seen $40 \div \frac{4}{3}$)
2 **a** $\frac{11}{20}$ **b** $4\frac{1}{24}$ **c** $1\frac{1}{2}$ **d** $1\frac{1}{3}$
3 **a** $\frac{3}{16}$ **b** $\frac{7}{12}$
4 5 cm (1 mark for $3\frac{1}{8}$ cm^2)
5 **a** $3\frac{11}{12}$ **b** $\frac{13}{15}$ **c** $2\frac{4}{5}$ **d** $2\frac{1}{6}$
6 **a** $\frac{4}{9}$ **b** $\frac{3}{5}$ **c** $\frac{6}{25}$
7 $17\frac{2}{5}$, 35
8 **a** $5\frac{3}{4}$ (1 mark for $3\frac{9}{20} \times 1\frac{2}{3}$)   **b** 3 (1 mark for $1\frac{1}{3} + 1\frac{2}{3}$)

Exercise 4 Percentages

1 **a** £70   **b** 75%   **c** £35
2 **a** North America
   b 60.7 or 61% (1 mark for $3737 \div 6157 \times 100$)
3 **a** 17.5%   **b** 116 the 115.3 need to be rounded up (1 mark for $17.5 \div 659 \times 100$)

Exercise 5 Percentage and proportional change

1 **a** 25   **b** 30
2 **a** 24.3 miles (1 mark for 6.3)   **b** 22.2% (1 mark for digits 222)
3 **a** $4.59   **b** £17.50   **c** €434 (1 mark for $558 \div 180 \times 140$)
4 **a** £64 (1 mark if $40 \times \frac{160}{100}$ or equivalent seen)
   b 2 weeks – 1 month (1 mark for $44.2 \div 68$)
5 **a** £216 (1 mark for $15 \times \frac{1440}{100}$)
   b 12% (1 mark for $1282 \div 10682$)
6 **a** 0.14×56 **b** 1.56×14 **c** 1.15
7 29.5% (1 mark for $162\,925 \div 552\,479$ $(= 0.2948\ldots)$)

Exercise 6 Harder percentages

1 **a** 60×0.96 **b** 1.13
2 £16 000 (1 mark for $20\,000 \div 1.25$)
3 **a** 6000×1.08^2 **b** $£p \times 1.10 \times 0.88$
4 $100 \times 1.10 \times 1.20 = 1.32 = 32\%$

5 **a**

Retailers	5.7% or 6%	(1 mark for two correct)
Taxes	70.1% or 70%	
Others	24.1% or 24%	

   b 85.7p (accept 86p) (1 mark for $6 \div 7 \times 100$)

Exercise 7 Ratio

1 **a** $1:3$ **b** $3:5$ **c** $2:7$ **d** $3:4$
2 **a** $1:3.5$ **b** $1:2.5$ **c** $1:1.6$ **d** $1:2.7$
3 750 g (1 mark if 250 seen)
4 **a** $7:8$ **b** 12
5 **a** £16 and £64 (1 mark if 16 seen)
   b 36 kg and 84 kg (1 mark if 12 seen)
6 9 squares shaded on the diagram (1 mark for showing $24 \div 8$)
7 100 oak trees, 200 beech trees and 300 sycamore trees (1 mark for showing $600 \div 6$)
8 **a** Hannah £24 and Jack £36 (1 mark for showing $60 \div 10$)
   b Hannah £25 and Jack £35 (1 mark for showing $60 \div 12$)
9 $1:2$ (1 mark for black area = 12 and 1 mark for grey area = 24)
10 **a** $3:5$ **b** $5:8$
   c The large tin (1 mark for showing, for small tin, 1p for 9.6 g. 1 mark for showing, for large tin, 1p for 10 g)

Exercise 8 Powers and roots

1 **a** 128   **b** 729   **c** 100 000 000
2 **a** 4^8 **b** 5^6 **c** 7^{12}
3 $3^{-2} = \frac{1}{9}$, $3^0 = 1$, $\sqrt[3]{27} = 3$, $\sqrt[3]{125} = 5$, $2^4 = 16$
   (1 mark for each number in correct position)
4 **a** $x = \pm 4$ (1 mark for 4)   **b** $x = \pm 10$ (1 mark for 10)
   c $x = \pm 3$ (1 mark for 3)
5 **a** $x = 4$ **b** $x = 3$ **c** $x = 2$
6 **a** $3^4 = 81$ (1 mark for 3 correct from 32, 81, 64, 25, 6)   **b** 4^3
7 **a** $a = 2, b = 4$ **b** $m = 3, n = 2$
8 **a** n^2 **b** $\sqrt{n}$ **c** 1
9 0 and 1
10 **a** 6 and 7   **b** 9 and 10   **c** 14 and 15
11 4.6 m
12 **a** For example: $\sqrt{9} \times \sqrt{16} = \sqrt{144} = 12$ (1 mark for substituting 2 different numbers)
   b For example: $\sqrt{9} + \sqrt{16} = 7 \neq \sqrt{25}$ (1 mark for substituting 2 different numbers)

Exercise 9 Standard form

1 **a** 1.412×10^6 km
   b 3.288×10^6 km (accept answers to 2 or 3 sf)
2 **a** 2.5×10^{-4} **b** 2.5×10^{-5} **c** 2.75×10^{-4}
3 **a** Asia   **b** Europe
   c Africa, since Africa has 26.8 people/km^2 and North America has 19.8 people/km^2. (1 mark for 26.8, 1 mark for 19.8 and 1 mark for correct conclusion)
4 1.94×10^{17} (1 mark if not rounded to 3 sf)
5 **a** **i** The distance of the Earth's orbit in miles
   ii The speed of the Earth around the Sun in mph
   b 66 700

Exercise 10 Number patterns and generalisation

1 **a** Column 3   **b** 46   **c** $5n - 2$ **d** Row 7
2 **a** 10001   **b** $n^2 + 1$ **c** 29

3 $H = 5M + 1$

4 a i $n^2 - n + 1 + 1 = n^2 - n$ **ii** $n^2 - n + 1 - 1 = n^2 - n$
  b $12^2 - 12 + 1 = 144 - 12 + 1 = 133$ **c** n^2

Exercise 11 Formulae and equations with powers

1 a -0.4 **b** 8 or 12 (1 mark for each value)

2 a i 41.25 m   **ii** 13 m/s   **b i** -7 m/s^2 **ii** It is slowing down.

3 a P = $33\frac{1}{3}$ cm   A = $29\frac{4}{9}$ cm^2 (1 mark for each value)
  b P = 19.06 cm   A = 5.32 cm^2 (1 mark for each value)
  c P = $14\frac{2}{3}t$, A = $6t^2 - \frac{4}{9}t$ (1 mark for each value)

4 i V = 73.3 cm^3 S = 185.8 cm^2 (1 mark for each value)
  ii V = $24\pi a^3$ cm^3 S = $32\pi a^2$ cm^2 (1 mark for each value)

5 a $3n$ and $\frac{n}{0.2}$ (1 mark for each value)
  b $\sqrt[3]{n}$ and n^3 (**1 m**ark for each value)   **c** n^3

Exercise 12 Solving linear equations

1 a The number of red and green pencils is 11.
  b The number of blue pencils is three times the number of red pencils.
  c There are 17 more blue pencils than green pencils.

2 a $p = 2$ **b** $m = 3$ **c** $y = 6$ (1 mark for $2y = 12$)
  d $x = -\frac{1}{2}$ (1 mark for $2x = -1$)

3 $x = 4.5$ (1 mark), length = 20.5 cm, width = 2 cm

4 $x = 3$ (1 mark for $x + 10 + x - 4 = 4x$)

5 a $3x - 7 = 23$, $x = 10$ **b** 11

Exercise 13 Linear and simultaneous equations

1 a Perimeter of first rectangle: $2(y + 3) + 2(x + 2) = 20$,
    $2y + 2x + 10 = 20$ (1 mark for $2y + 2x = 10$, $y + x = 5$)
    Perimeter of second rectangle: $2(2x) + 2(4y - 3) = 20$,
    $4x + 8y - 6 = 20$ (1 mark for $4x + 8y = 26$, $2x + 4y = 13$)
  b $x = 3.5$, $y = 1.5$ (1 mark each)

2 a $3y = 6x + 9$ (1 mark), $x = 2.5$ (1 mark), $y = 8$ (1 mark)

3 a $3(2x + 5) = x + 5$ **b** $x = -2$ **c** $y = 1$

4 a 7   **b** $4z - 3 = 9z + 12$ (1 mark), $z = -3$ (1 mark)

5 $12y - 4 = 6y$ (1 mark), $y = \frac{2}{3}$ (1 mark)

6 $4a = 6$ (1 mark), $a = 1.5$ (1 mark), $b = 10$ (1 mark)

7 a $8x - 4 = 3x + 6$ (1 mark), $x = 2$ (1 mark)
  b $3y - 2 = 8y + 12$ (1 mark), $y = -2.8$ (1 mark)
  c $3z + 2 = 7z$ (1 mark), $z = 0.5$

8 $x = £2.60$ (1 mark), $y = £1.20$ (1 mark), $2x + y = £6.40$

9 $3x + 4y = 4450$, $2x + 3y = 3250$ (1 mark), $x = £3.50$ (1 mark), $y = £8.50$ (1 mark)

Exercise 14 Combining and rearranging algebraic expressions

1 a $x + 5$, $y + 5$, $x + y + 10$ **b** $2x + 1$, $4x + 3$, $4x + 2$

2 $3x - 1$, $2x + 3$

3 a $6x - 2$ **b** $3x + 3$ **c** $x - 3$

4 a $a = \frac{x}{3} - b$ or $a = \frac{x - 2b}{3}$ (1 mark for $3a = x - 3b$ or $\frac{x}{3} = a + b$)
  b $b = a - 3x$ (1 mark for $3x = a - b$)

5 a $r(\pi + 2)$ **b** $r = \frac{P}{\pi + 2}$ (1 mark for $P = r(\pi + 2)$)

6 $r = \sqrt{\frac{3V}{\pi h}}$ (1 mark for $r^2 = \frac{3V}{\pi h}$)

7 a $x = \sqrt[3]{\frac{V}{6}}$ (1 mark for $x^3 = \frac{V}{6}$)   **b** 4.4 cm

8 a $-3(x - 2)$ or $-3x + 6$ (1 mark for $2y = 12 - 6x$)
  b $y = 2x + 9$ (1 mark for $3y = 6x + 27$)

9 a $u = v - at$ **b** $u = \sqrt{v^2 - 2as}$ (1 mark for $u^2 = v^2 - 2as$)

10 a $r = \sqrt[3]{\frac{3V}{4\pi}}$ (1 mark for $r^3 = \frac{3V}{4\pi}$)   **b** 2.9 cm

Exercise 15 Expansion of brackets

1 a $a^2 + 9a + 18$ (1 mark for two correct terms)
  b $b^2 - 3b - 4$ (1 mark for two correct terms)
  c $c^2 + c - 42$ (1 mark for two correct terms)
  d $4d^2 - 21d + 20$ (1 mark for two correct terms)
  e $9e^2 - 12e + 4$ (1 mark for two correct terms)
  f $15 - f - 6f^2$ (1 mark for two correct terms)

2 a $(x + 4)(x + 6)$ **b** $2y^2 + 17y - 9$ (1 mark for two correct terms)

3 A = $\frac{1}{2}(p + 10)(p + 6) = \frac{1}{2}(p^2 + 16p + 60) = \frac{1}{2}p^2 + 8p + 30$
  (1 mark for correct expansion)

4 a $2n^2$ cm^2, $12n$ cm^2, $3n$ cm^2, 18 cm^2 (1 mark for two correct terms)
  b $2n^2 + 15n + 18$

5 It should be $9x^2 + 30x + 25$ (1 mark for two correct terms)

6 a $(x + y)(x - y) = x^2 - xy + xy - y^2 = x^2 - y^2$ (1 mark for correct expansion)
  b i 35   **ii** 800   **iii** 1200

Exercise 16 Factorising

1 $2a^2b^2$ and $18ab$

2 a $3(4a + 20) = 2(6a + 30)$ **b** $5(4b - 1)$

3 $3y^2(y - 6)$ as it is equivalent to $3y^3 - 18y^2$. All the others are equivalent to $3y^3 - 9y^2$.

4 a $4(x + 3)$ **b** $5x^2(2x - 1)$

5 Both Alan and Beth are right as the two expressions are equivalent.

6 Let integers be n, $n + 1$, $n + 2$
  $n + n + 1 + n + 2 = 3n + 3 = 3(n + 1)$, which is a multiple of 3 (1 mark for $3n + 3$)

7 a $4n + 6$ **b** $2(2n + 3)$
  c $4n + 6 = 2(2n + 3)$, which is a multiple of 2, therefore even.

Exercise 17 Substitution

1 a 41   **b** 14   **c** 11.25

2 a 14   **b** 2   **c** 0.56

3 a 32°F   **b** 212°F   **c** 98.8°F (1dp)   **d** 17.6°F

4 a 16.5p (accept 17p) (1 mark for $330 \div 20$)
  b $2\frac{1}{2}$ minutes (1 mark for showing $180 = t + 30$)

5 a £52.50 (1 mark for $25.5 + 27$)
  b 4 (1 mark for showing $35 = 17 + 4.5c$)

6 a 55   **b** 1275   **c** 500 500

7 a 18.4 m/s (1 mark for showing $100 + 240$)
  b 37.9 m/s (1 mark for showing $1600 - 160$)

Exercise 18 Proof and explanation

1 a False, it is always even: $3(3 + 1) = 12$, $2(2 + 1) = 6$
  b True, at least one of the numbers must be even:
    $3(3 + 1)(3 + 2) = 60$
  c True, if n is even, $n^2 + 1$ is odd; if n is odd $n^2 + 1$ is even:
    $2^2 + 1 = 5$, $3^2 + 1 = 10$

2 a When x is odd x^2 is odd because odd × odd = odd.
  b When x is odd $(x - 1)(x + 1)$ is even as both brackets are even and even × even = even.

3 Calculation is approximately $\frac{40 \times 55}{30 - 10} = \frac{2200}{20} \approx 110$ so the answer is 'Right'. (2 marks for 110, 1 mark for $2200 \div 20$)

4 a Any value of x which is greater than 0 but less than 1.
  b $x = 0$ or 1   **c** Any value of x less than 0 or greater than 1.

5 a 1080°. An octagon can be split into six triangles.
    $6 \times 180 = 1080°$
  b The statement is true because the polygon splits into two fewer triangles than the number of sides (1 mark) and the angle sum of each triangle is 180° (1 mark).

6 a It is not possible to make a triangle because the two smaller sticks, when put together, are still shorter than the longest stick.

b Assume the equal sides are 1, then the sides are 1, 1, 11 which won't make a triangle.

This is also the case with 2, 2, 9 and 3, 3, 7. But if the equal sides are 4 or 5 then the triangle is 4, 4, 5 or 5, 5, 3, and 6, 6, 1, all of which obey all three rules.

Exercise 19 Graphs of linear equations

1 a Yes, because $2 \times 20 + 1 = 41$ **b** (2.5, 6)

c $y = 2x + c$, where c is any value except 1

2 a

Number of people	0	10	20	30
Total cost of admission	0	£51	**£102**	**£153**

b

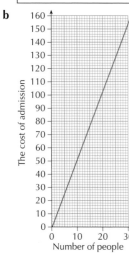

The cost of admission vs Number of people

c £127.50 (allow £127–£128)

(1 mark for plotting points)

3 a A: $x = 1$, B: $y = x + 1$, C: $y = 6$, D: $x + y = 4$

b A and B, because $y = 2x$ also has the coordinates (1, 2)

Exercise 20 Graphs from real-life

1 a Ann **b** Beryl, 5 minutes **c** 7 minutes

d 9 minutes **e** Beryl overtook Ann.

2 Graph C

3
 a **b** **c**

Exercise 21 Solving inequalities

1 a $-1 < x < 2$ **b** $-1 \leq x \leq 4$ **c** 0 or 1

2 a $x = 3$ **b** $x > 3$ **c** $x < -3$

3

	$x + y > 4$	$x + y < 4$
$y > x$	A	B
$y < x$	D	C

4 a $-6 \leq n \leq 6$ **b** $-10 < n < 10$

5 a $n \geq 3$ or $n \leq -3$ **b** $n > 5$ or $n < -5$

6 a $x > 18$ **b** $x \leq 2$ **c** $x > -1$

Exercise 22 Compound measures

1 1.6 m/s (1 mark for showing 125 s)

2 40 km/h (1 mark for finding time = 2.5 hours)

3 6 litres (1 mark for showing 90 km)

4 a 6 km/h **b** 30 minutes **c** 4 km/h

5 a 40 mph **b** 52 mph **c** 48 mph

6 3 hours 20 minutes (1 mark for showing 200)

Exercise 23 Angles in a polygon

1 $a = 180 - 75 = 105°$ $b = 180 - 25 = 155°$ $c = 180 - 80 = 100°$

2 $x = 180 - 85 = 95°$ $y = (360 - (3 \times 85)) \div 3 = 35°$

3 Each angle in an equilateral triangle is 60°, hence $a = 60°$
$b = 180 - 60 = 120°$

4 a $(4 - 2) \times 180 = 360°$ **b** $(6 - 2) \times 180 = 720°$

5 a Any of PBA, PAB, ARD **b** Any of DAB, ADR

c $180 - 75 - 65 = 40°$

6 a $((5 - 2) \times 180) \div 5 = 108°$ **b** $108 - 90 = 18°$

c $(180 - 108) \div 2 = 36°$

Exercise 24 Pythagoras' theorem

1 9.8 km (2 marks for 9.76***, where *** can be anything), (1 mark for 95.29)

2 12.49 cm (1 mark for $16^2 - 10^2$ or 156)

3 11.31 cm (2 marks for 11.31***, where *** can be anything), (1 mark for 128)

4 $5^2 + 12^2 = 25 + 144 = 169$, $13^2 = 169$, hence $5^2 + 12^2 = 13^2$, so a right-angled triangle (1 mark for 169)

5 325 m (1 mark for 105 300)

Exercise 25 Trigonometry

1 No, using sine and the sides given, the angle 28 should be 38.7°. (2 marks for getting to $\sin^{-1} = \frac{5}{8}$, 1 mark for stating $\sin x = \frac{5}{8}$)

2 The height of the trapezium is given by $20\tan75 = 74.64$ cm

So the area $= \frac{74.64}{2}(125 + 85) = 7837$ cm².

(2 marks for getting to 74.64, 1 mark for getting a right-angled triangle with a base of 20)

3 a base $= 2\cos3° = 1.997$ m

(2 marks for base $= 2\cos3$, 1 mark for $\frac{base}{2} = \cos3$)

b $\sin\theta = \frac{1}{20} = 0.05$, $\sin^{-1}, 0.05 = 2.9°$

(2 marks for $\sin^{-1} 0.05$, 1 mark for $\sin\theta = \frac{1}{20}$)

4 One of the equal angles is the smallest, call it x, then $\cos x = \frac{3.5}{5} = 0.7$, $\cos^{-1} 0.7 = 45.6°$

(2 marks for $\cos^{-1} 0.7$, 1 mark for $\cos x = \frac{3.5}{5}$)

Exercise 26 Circumference and area of a circle

1 30.85 cm (1 mark for 18.85 cm)

2 a 113.1 cm **b** 8840 times (1 mark for 1 000 000 cm)

3 Yes, with full justification, e.g. Circumference is 785.4, $785.4 \div 75 > 10$. (2 marks for $785.4 \div 75$, 1 mark for 785.4)

4 157.1 cm² (1 mark for 314.2 cm²)

5 6.8 cm² (2 marks for $\pi \times 1.9^2 - \pi \times 1.2^2$, 1 mark for either $\pi \times 1.9^2$ or $\pi \times 1.2^2$)

6 a 81.7 cm **b** 6.9 cm (1 mark for 47.7)

7 5.6 cm (2 marks for 2.8 cm, 1 mark for $25 \div \pi$)

8 4.5 cm (1 mark for $28 \div 2\pi$)

9 64% (2 marks for $200 \div 314.2 \times 100$, 1 mark for 314.2)

Exercise 27 Circles, sectors and cylinders

1 a $4\pi a^2$ (1 mark for $(\pi) \times (3a)^2 \div 2 - (\pi) \times a^2 \div 2$

b $a = 0.977 = 1.0$ (1 mark for $a^2 = 3 \div \pi$)

2 2 (1 mark for $\pi r^2 = 2\pi r$)

3 1.5 minutes (1 mark for $6.28 \div 250$)

4 1.5 cm (1 mark for $100\pi h = 150\pi$)

5 a i $\frac{1}{6}$ **ii** $\frac{1}{5}$

b 60° sector has area of 33.5 cm², 72° sector has area 30.78 cm². (1 mark for either value)

c 60° sector has perimeter of 24.4 cm, 72° sector has perimeter of 22.8 cm. (1 mark for either value)

d 4.1 cm (2 marks for 4.0915, 1 mark for $r = (5\pi + 10) \div 2\pi$)

6   40 200 km (1 mark for $2\pi \times 6400$)

7   Cylinder A has volume 565.5 cm³, Cylinder B has volume 235.6 cm³. (1 mark for either value)

8   367.6 cm³ (1 mark for $\pi \times 8^2 \times 3 - \pi \times 5^2 \times 3$)

9   Area $= \frac{1}{10} \times \pi \times 10^2 = \frac{1}{10} \times 100\pi = 10\pi$. (1 mark for $\frac{1}{10} \times \pi \times 10^2$)

10 4.37 cm (1 mark for $60 = \pi r^2$)

Exercise 28   Area of plane shapes

1   A (area of rectangle and parallelogram = 12 cm², triangle = 6 cm²)

2   Any triangle with an area of 6 cm², e.g. triangle base = 6 cm, height = 2 cm

3   B, C and D

4   **a** 6 cm (1 mark for area = 36)   **b** 18 cm (1 mark for $2y = 36$)

Exercise 29   Volume of 3-D shapes

1

3	2	4
3	1	8
2	2	6
4	1	6

2   **a** 48 cm³ (1 mark if units not stated)   **b** $x = 8$

3   **a** 750 m³ (1 mark for showing area of trapezium = 75 m²)
    b 750 000 litres

4   320 cm³ (1 mark for showing cross-sectional area is 40 cm²)

5   385 cm³ (1 mark for showing the calculation: $\pi \times 3.5^2 \times 10$)

Exercise 30   Congruent and similar shapes

1   **a** B and C. All sides are the same length.
    b A and E. The corresponding sides are in the same ratio.

2   9

3   6.4 cm (1 mark for the ratio $\frac{BD}{8} = \frac{20}{25}$)

4   **a** The ratio for the heights and diameters are not the same or 8:10 = 4:5, but 6:8 = 3:4.
    b 9 cm

Exercise 31   Transformations

1   **a** and **c** Check diagram
    b 90°

(1 mark for each correct vertex)

3   $a = 4$, $b = 5$ and $c = 120$

4   **a** (0, 8)   **b** B'(−2, 4), C'(2, 4)

5   **a** (−1, 5)
    b

(1 mark for any enlargement of scale factor 1)

Exercise 32   Parallel lines

1   **a** 60°   **b** 50°   **c** 70°

2   **a** $3x$ **b** $4x = 180$ **c** $x = 45°$

3   The angle vertically opposite 115° is also 115°. This angle and angle x are allied angles, so they add up to 180°. Hence, $x = 180 − 115 = 65°$. (1 mark for $x = 65°$ with no explanation)

4   **a** The transversal will be perpendicular to the parallel lines.
    b The transversal will cut the parallel lines at an angle of 45°.

5   **a** 70°   **b** 45° (1 mark if 135° shown in working)

Exercise 33   Constructions and loci

1   Accurate drawing with lines within 1 mm and angle within 1 degree

2

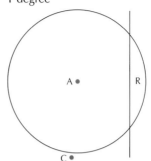

(1 mark for correct perpendicular bisector of BC with construction lines)
(1 mark for circle with radius 4 cm, centred on A)
(1 mark for correct position of R)

Exercise 34   Probability

1   **a** $\frac{35}{36}$ **b** $\frac{1}{36}$ **c** $\frac{6}{36} = \frac{1}{6}$

2   P(Toffee from A) = 25/40 = 0.625, P(Toffee from B) = $\frac{28}{50}$ = 0.56. Choose Tin A. (1 mark for each probability and 1 mark for correct conclusion)

3   The correct answer is $\frac{1}{5}$ because there are five discs in the bag and only one is blue.

4   The five numbers are 2, any two even numbers other than 2 and any two odd numbers (1 mark for three correct numbers)

5   **a**

              First card

+	1	2	3	4
1	2	3	4	5
2	3	4	5	6
3	4	5	6	7
4	5	6	7	8

Second card 2, 3, 4 (rows as above)

(1 mark for two correct columns or rows)

    b $\frac{5}{16}$ **c** $\frac{11}{16}$ **d** 0

Exercise 35   Relative frequency

1   $\frac{7}{8}$

2   **a** 12   **b** 40 (1 mark for 16 ÷ 0.4)
    c Possibly as P(Italian) = 0.3, but the sample is too small to be sure.

3   **a** **i** 0.3   **ii** 0.65   **b** 9
    c A girl as there are five times as many girls as boys

Exercise 36   Probability of combined events

1   Bag B. P(R in bag B) = $\frac{10}{16} = \frac{5}{8}$ (= $\frac{25}{40}$), P(R in bag A) = $\frac{3}{5}$ (= $\frac{24}{40}$)
    (1 mark if either probability of red worked out)

2   **a** 200   **b** $\frac{1}{400}$ (1 mark for $\frac{1}{20} \times \frac{1}{20}$)
    c $\frac{38}{400} = \frac{19}{200}$ = (1 mark if $\frac{1}{20} \times \frac{19}{20}$ written down)

3   **a** HTT, THH, THT, TTH, TTT   **b** P(H) × P(H) = $\frac{1}{2} \times \frac{1}{2}$
    c $\frac{1}{2}$ **d** $\frac{1}{8}$

4   **a** **i** $\frac{1}{6}$ **ii** $\frac{5}{6}$
    b **i** P(6) × P(6') + P(6') × P(6) = $\frac{1}{6} \times \frac{5}{6} + \frac{5}{6} \times \frac{1}{6} = \frac{10}{36}$
        (1 mark for P(6) × P(6') + P(6') × P(6))

ii $\frac{1}{36}$ **iii** lose £25 (1 mark for P(no sixes) = $\frac{25}{36}$)

Exercise 37 Surveys and questionnaires

1 **a** She is right because there are overlapping boxes. For
     example, a 10-year-old could tick two boxes.
   b Any reasonable labels that do not overlap. For example:
     ☐ £   ☐ £0.01–£4.99   ☐ £5.00–£9.99   ☐ £10 or over
   c i They will only get a sample from people aged 11 to 16 so
       it will not be representative.
     ii It will be easy to organise and the sample size is good.

2 Question 1 is good because it is relevant to the survey,
   responses cover all values and there are no overlapping
   responses.
   Question 2 is bad because there are two questions in one about
   fruit and vegetables and there are overlapping responses.

3 **a i** The sample may not be representative.
     ii It will be easy to organise and the sample size is big
       enough.
   b The sample is too small.
     The sample is not representative: they will probably pick
     sport as the favourite subject.

Exercise 38 Discrete and grouped data

1 38 (1 mark for total marbles = 12 × 36 = 432, 1 mark for total
   in 11 bags = 394)

2 **a** 1 × 13 + 2 × 23 + 3 × 16 + 4 × 5 + 5 × 4 = 147
   b 2.4 (1 mark for 147 ÷ 61)
   c 1010 (1 mark for 526 × 2.4 × 0.8)

3 **a** 37.8 cm (1 mark for total of 3780)
   b See right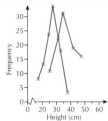
   c Smaller as the frequency polygon for the outside plants is to
     the left of the frequency polygon for the inside plants.

Exercise 39 Pie charts

1 **a** 60   **b** ii   **c** 60% of 50 = 30 members
   d Because in Avery YC 40% of 100 would play table tennis,
     which is 40 members. This is larger than the 30 at Banner
     Cross YC.

2 45% of the money is spent on education, 15% on health, 20%
   on social services and 20% on other. Angles in a pie chart total
   360° so you should therefore have a pie chart with angles of
   162° for education, 54° for health, and 72° each for social
   services and other. They should all be labelled. (1 mark if
   angles correct but incorrectly labelled)

3 **a** 72° is 20% of 360°. Therefore 20% of the students surveyed
     liked cats. 9 students liked cats so the total number of people
     surveyed is 9 × 5 = 45.
   b 104°
   c Does not divide by 8°, which is the angle per student.

Exercise 40 Scatter diagrams and lines of best fit

1 **a** Average daily takings increase with the size of the village
     (positive correlation).
   b There is no relationship between daily takings and distance
     to nearest supermarket.

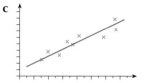

c

d £580–£620

2 **a** As the hours of sunshine increases, the rainfall decreases
     (negative correlation).
   b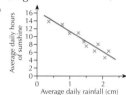
   c 13 hours
   d The graph is only valid up to 2 cm of rainfall.

3 **a** Maths and Science, weak positive correlation
     Maths and English, no correlation
   b Science and English, no correlation

Exercise 41 Median and mean

1 **a** 1.8 points
   b

Number of games won	7
Number of games drawn	2
Number of games lost	1

2 **a** $2x - 1$ **b** $4x - 3$ (1 mark for $8x - 6$)

3 **a** 1 × 1 + 2 × 6 + 3 × 9 + 4 × 11 + 5 × 3 = 2 + 10 + 27 + 44 +
     15 = 99
   b 99 peas = 30 pods = 3.3 peas per pod
   c 28, 29 or 30 (1 mark for 1000 peas ÷ 35 = 28.57 meals)

4 173 bottles (1 mark for 240 + 81 + 166 + 170 or 657)

5 **a**

Age group (years)	0–9	10–19	20–29
Mid value (x)	5	**15**	**25**
Frequency (f)	2	7	**11**

   b He is not correct. The median must be in the 20–29 age
     group as over half of the people are over 19.
   c 19 years (1 mark for (10 + 105 + 265) ÷ 20)

Exercise 42 Stem-and-leaf diagrams and box plots

1 **a** 18   **b** 9   **c** 40   **d** 25   **e** 25   **f** 6

2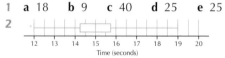

   Note that the box around the median can be anywhere as long
   as it is 1.5 seconds long.
   Take a mark off for any wrong values plotted.

3 **a** 4 grams   **b** May by 1 gram   **c** In May just come out of
     hibernation, or in October feeding up ready for winter.

Exercise 43 Cumulative frequency

1 **a** 2.3 hours   **b** 1.4 hours (1 mark for UQ = 3 and LQ = 1.6)
   c Mark can be awarded for any valid comment e.g. Generally
     people spent longer at the theme park and the length of time
     spent was more consistent or less varied.

2 (1 mark for each correct statement)
   e.g. Median less for girls, on average, smaller than boys
   Interquartile range less for girls (girls' heights more consistent)
   Range less for girls